OVERBURDEN

Modern Life
on the Iron Range

Long live the Range!

Aaron Brown

RED STEP PRESS

Duluth, Minnesota

RED DIRT AND OVERBURDEN
Modern Life on the Iron Range
by Aaron Brown

Red Step Press
Post Office Box 7103
Duluth, MN 55703
www.redsteppress.com

Cover photo by Kelly O'Brien
Cover design by Christie Culliton

ISBN 10: 0980078903
ISBN 13: 9780980078909

PRINTED IN CANADA

FIRST EDITION

For Henry, Douglas and George,
who inspired this book;

and for Christina, who inspires me.

Table of Contents

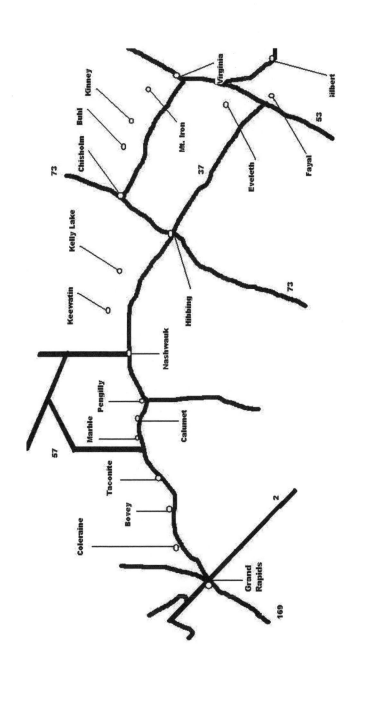

Special thanks to the *Hibbing Daily Tribune* and KAXE 91.7 Radio in Grand Rapids for permission to reprint many of Aaron Brown's columns in this book.

The reprinted pieces are noted in the text and appear with minor changes from their original form. These changes were made to maintain a consistent style in the book, and the overall integrity of the content of each piece was preserved.

Aaron's son Henry

Telling a Story

Up at the deer shack last year, I asked Grandpa Brown to tell me a story about working the underground iron ore mines here on the Iron Range. Grandpa leaned back in his squeaky deer shack chair, cupping a tumbler filled with half-Windsor, half-charged water.

"There's water running all the time," he said. "You hear this dripping the whole time you're down there, and at first it makes you nervous. But if that water ever stops, you've got seconds to get out. Seconds. Because it's all coming down. You don't want to hear silence down in the mine."

This tiny detail connected different ideas I've been having about the Iron Range, its history and future, its people, and its problems. But mostly, it served to remind me of my family's place here. We were here then. We're here now. We'll be here tomorrow. And everyone has a story.

Each night, Christina and I read bedtime stories to our boys. *Curious George. Thomas the Tank Engine. Goodnight Moon. Time for*

Bed. If you're not a big reader of kid's stories, here's all you need to know. Take deep human emotions – love, loss, fear, or anger – and mix them with comically implausible situations. Talking trains teach my kids about working together. A monkey that would probably be in jail for destruction of property reminds the boys that we should always be curious about the world around us. But unique characters and odd situations aren't the only thing needed for a good story. There is also the matter of setting.

It occurs to me that my sons will grow up as the sixth generation of my family on the Iron Range of northern Minnesota. This working class mining region has been the setting of my family's story. It's an implausible place, where implausible things keep happening. I am the unlikely son of miners, mechanics, and engineers, who now makes a living off writing, teaching, and the Internet.

I wonder how my boys will handle the burden faced by all Iron Rangers; how to navigate a hard, old place in a modern world. I wonder if they will learn to love this place as I have and if the efforts of today's generation will do any good for the next. I wonder if they will sleep through the night and what raucous discoveries they'll make in the morning. Kids live their lives in stories. Stories seep into their dreams, and their dreams will define them as adults.

Here is my story of growing up during an unglamorous time in Iron Range history. It's about riding out the Information Age in a place that just recently realized that dial-up Internet was slow. It's the story of how I learned to love a land defined by the people who came before and the people who remain. It's a story that belongs to everyone willing to work in the red shadow of overburden.

An overburden pile

A Place Called the Iron Range

You can learn a lot about a place from its dirt. Heartland dirt is rich, dark, and fertile. Desert dirt is rough and dry. City dirt is unremarkable and resigned to its role of holding up the pavement where humans do business.

On the Minnesota Iron Range, our dirt bleeds red from iron ore. Dry Iron Range dirt billows up in clouds around your legs, covering your clothing with dust that you can never brush off. Wet Iron Range dirt splashes deep red stains that will not be dispatched by traditional detergents. Pants, skirts, your skin itself: these will be red forever after walking in the shadow of the overburden piles where the mines dump their unused earth.

Like everywhere else in North America, the Iron Range started as a wilderness, until people came – first natives, then European explorers, trappers, loggers, and miners. These peoples became more than the population of the Iron Range; they blended with the landscape. They became like trees or rocks. Every generation found something special about this land that they didn't expect when they first arrived. It was this very specific land, *this place*, that provided their reason for being here.

I am an Iron Ranger. This title is one part geography and one part attitude. It's like saying, "I'm mad as hell and I'm not going to take it anymore," if Madzhellnotgontakeitanymore was a town about eighty miles north of Duluth and 200 miles north of Minneapolis. The names of our towns contain far fewer letters.

- Mountain Iron: The first town on the Mesabi Iron Range (one of several iron ranges in the area).
- Hibbing: My birthplace, where mining bosses poured money into city coffers to get the entire place moved three miles to the south.
- Eveleth: If you've never been to the Iron Range, you might have heard about this town in connection with hockey or a landmark sexual harassment lawsuit. Most folks would prefer to talk hockey.
- Ely: Gateway to the Boundary Waters Canoe Area and a point on the Vermilion Iron Range. Ely is a good example of what happens when a town full of isolated ex-miners is populated by neo-hippies. Add organic foods, guitars, and hunting supplies. Welcome to Ely.
- Grand Rapids: Representing the western edge of the Iron Range, Grand Rapids residents often spurn the label "Iron Range," even though their history is intertwined with their eastern neighbors. The debate continues.

Virginia, Gilbert, Buhl, Chisholm, Aurora, Babbitt, Hoyt Lakes, Biwabik, Bovey, Embarrass, Coleraine, Taconite, Keewatin, Tower, Nashwauk, Soudan, Pengilly, Calumet, Marble, Crosby, Ironton and others round out the list. Then there are the townships, the square geographical units created by a mapmaker during the state's pioneer stage. French, Balkan, Lavele, McDavitt, Cherry, Clinton, Fayal, Angora, Great Scott, and many more. To an Iron Ranger, these are familiar names.

Most Minnesotans know where "The Range," or colloquially "Da' Range" is, if only that it's somewhere "up north" and features a wide variety of "characters" who drive poorly on freeways. Some Minnesotans know the Range as a region of political and economic importance to the whole state. Still, for most people it remains mysterious. The Iron Range is not a population center. In fact, we've been steadily losing population since I was born in 1979, though at one time, it was the fastest growing and wildest part of the state. Many who live in today's fast growing Minneapolis/St. Paul (the "Twin Cities") suburbs and exurbs have roots on the Iron Range.

Geologically, the Iron Range is a series of iron formations drawn across a west-southwest to east-northeast line in northeastern Minnesota. Most of our cities, founded as mining towns, rest along this line, but none are bigger than a population of about 18,000 (Hibbing, our biggest city) with many hovering around 1,000 people. The total population of the Iron Range region is similar in size to Duluth, with a population of just under 100,000. Duluth is a midsized media market with a fairly diverse economy, though still more dependent on manufacturing and natural resources than is generally preferred. The Iron Range, despite the desperate hopes and claims of our chambers of commerce, remains almost completely dependent on natural resources, especially steel and wood products. As a result, our other industries remain equally volatile. The most consistent industry, which also employs the most people, is the medical sector. This serves the large population of aging and retiring miners, industrial workers, and their spouses. Most people are somewhere in the middle or lower economic classes. It's more of a stigma to be rich here than it is to be poor.

When I talk about the Iron Range, I usually talk about the ways it is different from your typical rural American region. Many of our towns have more Chinese restaurants than they do book stores. Some of our smallest towns have five places to buy alcohol, four places to buy bait, three places to worship Jesus, two places to gradually die in hospital beds, one place to join the Steelworkers union off the street, and nowhere, absolutely nowhere, to buy pants. Most Rangers are somewhat conservative, but they overwhelmingly vote Democratic. The area is deeply skeptical of outsiders, but at one time, it housed one of the most diverse immigrant populations in the country. When I started this project, I aimed to explain what the Iron Range is, both for a new generation of natives and a vast sea of foreign people who mistakenly think that our odd red bluffs and deep scarred canyons were made by God. The people here now do not depend on the land like our ancestors did. Thus, the Iron Range has become more people than place. If this place can be explained, and that's a dubious task for any book, it can only be done by meeting the people and listening to their stories.

This book is mostly a personal journey through a place I love, despite its flaws, and for which I hold great hope. I'll also be sharing some of my columns from the *Hibbing Daily Tribune* and my commentaries from KAXE, Northern Community Radio.

I've been a writer, reporter, and political organizer on the Iron Range since I earned my driver's license and drove my first car, a 1980 GM Cutlass Cruiser station wagon with three .22 caliber bullet holes in the driver's side door. At the time I write this, I am twenty-eight, no longer a kid, but far younger than the average age on the Iron Range. I am also far past the age when most educated young people are, in our culture, supposed to leave this area for big cities and suburbs, returning only to visit and bury their parents. Though I was out of the area for brief stints in Superior,

Wisconsin, and Dubuque, Iowa, most of my life and career has been spent near the ridge of the Mesabi Range iron formation. I expect a working majority of the rest of my life will be spent here, too.

I've been a radio announcer in Eveleth, a newspaper editor and college instructor in Hibbing, and one job in Virginia had me visit almost every public and nonprofit worksite in the seven counties of northeastern Minnesota. I've also done political work in every legislative district and almost every town north of Duluth and east of Bemidji. I mention this only to show that I've dug deep in the crannies of this place.

Sometime shortly after my oldest son was born, my thoughts drifted to my late great-grandfather, Ward George Brown, the first Brown to be born on the Mesabi Iron Range. He died two months after I was born. I never knew him, but he knew before he died that the Brown name would continue in northern Minnesota (Not that our last name, among the most common in the English-speaking world, is in any danger of dying out). He was a mining engineer who, by the end of his career, was leading some of the last of the underground iron ore mining operations in Minnesota on the Cuyuna Range. My grandfather and father were named for him. My great-grandfather was described to me as a good deal more proper and gentlemanly than most members of the family, who have come to merge the philosophies of intellectualism and the teachings of "Larry the Cable Guy." If it weren't for the relative unpopularity of the name "Ward," my name would have been Ward George Brown IV, an outcome that would have changed my life in many incalculable ways.

If the Browns had continued on their pattern of chasing ore across the world, we'd probably have moved away some time ago – somewhere with a booming mining economy like Brazil or Argentina. Though my ancestry is mixed with many different stories, the central line of the Brown family followed heavy mining operations through at least nine generations and three countries. The Browns came from Cornwall, England, where they probably mined tin and lead. Francis Lobb Brown left for Canada to mine iron ore before following the red rush to the Upper Peninsula of Michigan for copper and iron. A couple generations later, William Henry Brown came to the Mesabi Range for mining purposes, and every Brown until me has spent at least a small time working in an iron mine. My great-grandfather, Ward, and my grandfather, Ward Jr., worked some of the last underground mines on the Mesabi and Cuyuna Ranges. My father, Ward III, spent a short time working at a taconite plant.

I'm the first American member on either side of my family to *never* have worked in a mine or related field. Even so, I've chosen not to break those bonds between the Browns and the Iron Range.

I've made a conscious decision to stay despite numerous opportunities to leave. Now I have a family. My wife Christina grew up here, but her family is from northern Illinois originally. That makes ours a mixed marriage on the Iron Range. My sons Henry, born in 2005, and Doug and George, born in 2007, were delivered in Hibbing. My sons may be even more disconnected from the region's mining industry during their childhood. Even if they want to become miners when they're older, the industry in 2025 will require at least as much college education as being a teacher: I grew up around adults who had the option of working at the mines with a high school diploma or less. What else will be different for my sons? That is the great question of this place.

As a native Ranger, I know my homeland often carries a reputation as a rough and tumble industrial area on the decline. Our many chambers of commerce try to combat this with statistics about our growing medical community or vast tracts of tax free land. In truth, the Iron Range is as human a place as I've seen in all my travels. It's a place where people and land converge, and history happens.

I pose these questions. What is the Iron Range? What is the future of this place? Why shouldn't ambitious people like me, my wife, my friends, and many of my students leave this place to be overrun by closed-mindedness, regret, poverty, and old folks' homes?

Why does this place matter at all?

It does. It should. It will.

Last Ore Shipment from Bulter Taconite with Jerry Drong, Milan Basich, and Bill Shea—1985 (Photo courtesy Ironworld)

From Pine Tree to Broom: The Present History of the Iron Range

Part One

People came to the Iron Range long before anyone thought to make steel. Back in prehistoric times, there weren't any mine bosses to complain about or foreign cars to curse. From the natives who first populated the old thick forests, to the people who would later cut down the forests to build carts to carry out the iron ore, we Rangers have shared at least one important trait. The people who called this place home were survivalists. "Survival" is an important word here on the Iron Range, maybe the most important. No one ever had an easy time in the North Woods, and that shows up in our culture, art, and politics and throughout our historical narrative.

In the prime days of Iron Range mines, my great-grandfather and thousands like him dug underground for iron ore. When miners opened a fresh vein of ore, they stood a cut pine tree in the first lode of iron shipped to Duluth from the new mine. The companies then shipped the ore "Out East" to be made into steel. When a mine closed – and they all close eventually – miners would jam a broom into the last train car carrying ore out of the defunct mine. Then workers would sometimes board up the mine's opening. Often, the shafts were just abandoned until a child fell into one of them or the hole interfered with construction.

Long before I was born, when people here mined pure iron ore, this practice of displaying pine trees and brooms in the ore cars was common. Fortunes waxed and waned. Companies opened and closed mines along the jagged line of the Mesabi iron formation, reopened mines when a new vein was discovered later, or more likely, moved down the line to another new mine. Lots of pine trees. Lots of brooms.

In the 1950s, when Bobby Zimmerman (aka Bob Dylan) wandered downtown Hibbing with a guitar, the mines had finally depleted most of the Iron Range's accessible natural iron ore reserves. My grandfather Marvin Johnson left Keewatin to join the Air Force because of the lack of available mining jobs. He eventually returned to become a mine electrician. Meantime, the Browns, my grandfather and great-grandfather, were closing the last underground mines on the Mesabi and Cuyuna ranges. In the '50s, things looked pretty bad all over the Range. Lots of brooms, but no pine trees. It was before this time, in response to the waning ore supplies, that scientists developed the taconite process that would save this area from total economic destruction.

Taconite is a hard, lower-grade iron ore that, for more than fifty years prior, had been discarded as waste and used only as a signal that rich, natural ore might be nearby. The taconite process broke apart the hard rock, extracted the ore, and rolled it into pea-sized pellets that could be used in blast furnaces at eastern steel mills. In the 1960s and '70s, new taconite plants were built, and the first lodes of pellets carried the precious pine trees, each tree a sign of life and prosperity on the Iron Range. Each tree meant a good living for the hundreds who would mine and process the iron ore of this place.

In the 1980s, the Iron Range saw its first broom of the taconite age. Butler Taconite plant closed during a downturn in the steel market and a depression on the Range. Butler was located near Nashwauk, one of the places I lived as a little kid. My wife Christina went to elementary school in nearby Keewatin. During the first year after Butler closed, kids would just disappear from Christina's class, each moving with their family as their parents tried to find work.

Things picked up a bit in the 1990s – no pine trees, but no brooms either – until the end of the millennium. In 2001, LTV Steel closed its taconite mine and production plant in Hoyt Lakes. A picture of the broom in the last train car crossed the Associated Press photo wire when I was working at the *Hibbing Daily Tribune*.

So much about the history of the place where I grew up and now raise kids, is tied up in the trundling motions of these railroad pine trees and brooms. I suppose not everyone in my generation (the generation whose parents worked at Butler) knows about the pine trees and the brooms. In some ways, we're not much different from the twenty-somethings across America, with our beeping phonesy things and tickity-ticking on our computer Internets (note the trans-generational language). But unlike many youth, we are usually indoctrinated early in the cycle of economic ups and downs that makes the Iron Range what it is now. We all know at least part of our history.

You can't talk about the Iron Range without talking about history. Part of the reason history is so important here is because the most exciting human events of the region all happened within the lifetimes of people who still wander around downtown looking for free coffee. Growing up on the Iron Range in the 1980s was like living in the South during William Faulkner's youth. A young Billy Faulkner might have heard about "That Damned Ulysses Grant!" Young Iron Rangers like me heard about the damned mining companies, lawyers, politicians, and big shots promising better jobs in exchange for money. Unlike Grant in the South, however, the subjects of our Iron Range parents' cursing still do brisk business. The "Reconstruction" never ended on the Iron Range. It is thus no small irony that the Iron Range, heart of the industrial north in a state that provided the backbone of the Union defenses at Gettysburg, now sports an alarming number of trucks with confederate flags in the back window. We are still fighting the War of Eastern Aggression.

After the incorporation of our first towns, this area's existence fits snugly in five generations. When my grandparents tell me stories of *their* parents or grandparents, they tell me firsthand recollections about the beginning of the Iron Range. For modern Iron Rangers, history isn't just some dusty fact from an old book. Their mothers or fathers once sat in the laps of tired old men who mined the first red ore of this place. The founders of the Iron Range died not long ago. You can read about their kids in today's obituaries. Mining remains our dominant industry, and many of our miners do roughly the same job their great-grandfathers did, now with the aid of computers and sophisticated equipment. And there are far fewer miners working alongside them.

I talked to three historians, all native Iron Rangers, in my exploration of Iron Range history. Since I first made my decision to stay here and raise a family back in 1999, I have talked to just about anyone willing to share their Iron Range story. In piecing this information together, I have found a central theme. This place makes us who we are today. Our current population draws from forty-three different national origins and several great Native American tribes. Our geographic, economic, and sometimes self-imposed isolation created our cultural traditions, including our value of history, family, and rituals like hunting, fishing, going out on the town each Saturday and to church on Sunday (despite what was done Saturday).

Certainly the Iron Range is not homogenous, but it is curious how a place this important to our nation's industry and steel supply has remained so sociologically consistent over time. Most Rangers have a firm idea of what's fair and a willingness to speak out or act when needed. The problem with being as sure minded as Rangers tend to be, is that you fight just as hard when you're wrong as when you're right, and no one is right all the time. Rangers fought hard during the labor movement of the early 20th century and achieved great things for working people all over the world. We fought hard to build great schools. We fought to win a share of mining production revenue, which saved this region from complete economic collapse. At the same time, though, some Rangers also fought to keep women from working in the taconite mines during the 1970s and '80s, famously depicted in the book *Class Action* and the movie *North Country*. There has been corruption and cronyism. The early 20th century turned our towns into cauldrons of ethnic and labor violence. Time spent here reveals pockets of contempt for outsiders by a vocal and belligerent minority. Even many good people here fear change and hold dated views on matters of race, culture, and the world around us.

Isolation. Competition for limited resources. Cultural clashes. These things have defined Iron Range history and continue to shape our identity. On one side you've got pigheadedness, decline, and dependence on outside forces to change things. On the other you have hard-work, survival, and innovation.

I offer only an overview here from my own Iron Range history research and perspective. Anyone interested in the nitty-gritty of the Range's past should visit Ironworld and the Iron Range Research Center in Chisholm, the Hibbing Historical Center, or the other city and county historical societies across the Range. There are many talented historians working in the area. These people and places are the source of much of my knowledge of the region. I also recommend Marvin G. Lamppa's book *Minnesota's Iron Country*, which is the most comprehensive reference book on Iron Range history that I know of. It is fitting, perhaps, that no one Iron Range book or historical site could be considered definitive. Around every corner you find rich, unpublished details involving guns, spies, alcohol, religion, industrial espionage, conflict, politics, food, schools, and sometimes even cold-blooded murder. What is most important, is how longtime residents invoke Range history as they conduct present business. This history molded the last five of my family's generations and will shape the lives of my children.

A red dirt road

Highway 63 Revisited

Hibbing Daily Tribune, November 2007

They say the Iron Range is entering a modern age, a time of renaissance and progress. I have seen proof that this is true, but it has nothing to do with our impending new steel plant or nonferrous minerals. We've seen economic booms before, followed by busts and more booms. No, the proof of the modern age may be found on the highway from Hibbing to the locations.

Locations exist as one of the most interesting details you'll see on the Range. These small clusters of older, often symmetrical houses seem to orbit around our towns, especially around Hibbing – still the Range's largest town. Unlike the suburbs of Minneapolis and St. Paul, these locations don't hug the city limits, allowing drivers to pass the border unaware. Locations lie about a mile or more beyond their parent town on the other side of thick forests of trees and vast mines. Visitors may believe they are entering a new town – one with no apparent commerce, zoning regulations, or organized government of any kind. In truth, they enter a location. A place, yes, but not a town.

Locations formed around fast-growing mining operations at a time when there was no reliable means of public or personal transportation. Mine owners deemed it best for workers to live right at the mouth of the mine where access to drink, stores, and union organizers could be controlled. Companies quickly built these locations, assigning homes to the mostly immigrant workers who extracted the iron ore by pick, shovel, and hand.

As you drive west on a back road out of Hibbing proper, you pass through Kerr Location, Leetonia Location, and eventually Kelly Lake. In other directions, maps show evidence of older locations like Redore and Carson Lake, where former Governor Rudy Perpich and his family grew up, though mining activity has largely covered or blasted away their footprints.

I have always been fascinated by the location that once surrounded the ruins of the old Dupont blasting powder factory by Carey Lake, east of Hibbing. The factory reportedly blew up one day, creating the charred remains you can still see on the shore of the city's publicly owned lake. Surviving residents moved their location homes but left the foundations of a town that has since been absorbed by nature.

I work in Hibbing, but I live in the woods of Itasca County on the western Mesabi Range. There are two ways home; both take about half an hour if you don't encounter taconite trains or bad roads. The most obvious way is to take the freeway to Nashwauk and head north. My favorite way is to take Highways 63, 79, and 39, slipping stealthily into Itasca through Kerr and Leetonia locations and across the guts of Hibbing Taconite. I don't know of any drive that better shows the scars and beauty of the Iron Range.

They rerouted Highway 63 recently. A drive that once wound several ninety degree turns within a few feet of people's front porches, now bends widely around the locations, allowing increased speed and decreased awareness of these little towns that are not towns, not exactly.

On the old commute, my cell phone would always fly off the passenger seat of my car when I hit a turn too fast and roll around with the Diet Coke cans on the floor before I rescued it in time to avoid the oncoming traffic, usually a truck with the driver's name somehow affixed to a bug shield on the hood. I would momentarily flash back to the time when the roads were built, when mining trucks would rumble up the streets and no one used turn signals. It was a dangerous time but too new and exciting for anyone to know exactly how dangerous. Though I am a very modern Iron Ranger, complete with iPod and e-mail, the perilous turns on Highway 63 taught me what one can only learn in the shadows of these aging location houses. Not that long ago, Iron Rangers did not "log on"; they sawed logs. They did not mine data; they mined iron. And though these early Iron Rangers could have avoided many conflicts with the powerful moneyed interests that built the locations where they were told to live, they instead fought for fair wages, safer working conditions, and schools, schools, schools. Schools that taught me most of what I know.

This new route is safer and I welcome it, but I hope we remember the teachings of the old route as we pass the locations from a distance. As we all drive faster on this modern artery of progress, may we also remember all that is good about a life of hard work in a hard place.

Aaron's son Henry at Hull Rust Mine View in Hibbing

Being Young in an Old Place

Perhaps the problem that the Iron Range has with youth, shared by rural places all over the United States, is that young people are treated much the same way as pupae in an ant colony. They are well cared for, and protected, but, like ant pupae, they are distinctly separate, segregated often literally into other rooms within the colony. Our young often remain separate until a majority of the older people die. By then they are growing older and have chips on their shoulders for being held back so long.

It wasn't always this way. The old days were much simpler. During the dawn of the Iron Range, young people came of age when they were old enough to work somewhere: maybe a mine, a speakeasy, a brothel, a textile plant, or lighting arson fires for the International Workers of the World. As soon as the young people started working, they were old enough for everything else. The early part of the 20th century was full of leaders, business owners, and organizers who were in their twenties or thirties. Certainly there were plenty of middle aged folks, too, but the blend was much more reflective of the population.

Things have changed. No, not just here on the Iron Range, but anywhere that parents teach their children to look to big cities and suburbs for opportunity. Thus began the creation of two societies in rural places: those who feel too good to stay, and those who feel they aren't good enough to go. These are false concepts. Rural and small industrial places like the Iron Range have survived because of good people who stay. And I've watched plenty of morons leave for the big city. But the psyche remains. Good go; bad stay.

This became clearer to me when I began working at the *Hibbing Daily Tribune* shortly after I turned twenty-one. I had lived in Hibbing for a couple years at that point, commuting to and from Superior, Wisconsin, where I was attending college. Since I paid for college with a job as a radio reporter, it was relatively easy to find my way onto the Hibbing paper's staff. I was a beat reporter covering city politics and whatever else I could find. My goal at that time was to gain some experience, work my way up the ladder, and maybe get to be assistant editor in the next year or so. Ultimately, I wanted to be the editor of a Range daily. What I didn't know, or at least hadn't fully considered at the time, was that that the position of editor of the *Hibbing Daily Tribune* had become a modern Catch-22. It required all the critical thinking skills you'd expect, but also a good deal of mundane page layout and routine tasks. It paid a salary that was relatively good for a recent college graduate, by Iron Range standards at least, but not much when you considered the time required by the salaried position. As a result, no one had weighed down the editor's seat for more than two years in the previous decade. I was hired as a reporter just as one editor was leaving, and the position remained vacant while I settled into my routine, raising myself like a wolf boy in the wilderness of Iron Range journalism. Before long, I was laying out the front page, crafting issue stories, and trying to muscle my way onto the opinion page with a regular column.

When two or three editor candidates turned the position down after months of intensive advertising, the *Tribune's* then publisher, Terese Almquist, agreed to consider me for the position. In a process that took about a week, she decided to take a shot, and at twenty-one (and a half), I was the youngest editor in the paper's century-long history. The story crossed the AP wire, as is custom for new daily newspaper editors in Minnesota, and revealed my age. It was then that I learned that Terese thought I was several years older. "You're not really twenty-one, are you?" she asked me the next day. Yes I was. "Oh, wow," she said. She looked like someone who had just bought a haunted house.

Before you begin to worry that this is a self-aggrandizing passage, let me begin by saying that twenty-one-year-olds should not edit newspapers. While I was technically qualified to do the job, capable of handling the daily tasks and angry readers, the very fact that I was so young was a self-perpetuating problem. Each day, I had to explain to most people I encountered that, A) I was not twelve years old; B) that I really was capable of hearing what they had to say without zoning out to the crazy MTV; and C) I knew about things that happened before I was born, even though *I wasn't there*. Ultimately, that was what cranked up the stress levels to the point where graduate school and a teaching career seemed like a much better idea.

I realized that youth was a novelty on the Iron Range: special, perhaps interesting, and definitely unnatural to those who conduct the business of this place.

What We Teach Our Iron Range Children

"These are the lessons we teach our rural children today: that their parents were expendable and that their duty is to abandon their dreams and to become cogs in the industrial machine."
~Paul Gruchow*, from his 1995 essay
"What We Teach Rural Children"

Hibbing Daily Tribune, January 2002

Early in 2002, my wife and I heard Minnesota author, Paul Gruchow, read one of his essays at an event in Mountain Iron. Gruchow, a native of the farming region of southern Minnesota, specializes in the analysis of rural culture. He's a former small-town newspaper editor and has a perspective on the decline of population and culture in Minnesota's rural communities that resonates here on the Iron Range.

The economic problems facing the Iron Range are significant but not unlike those Gruchow remembers growing up in a farming community in the 1950s. He witnessed people go out of business or leave town, just as we do now. He saw consolidation and market forces eliminate farming jobs, just as they now prey on our mining and manufacturing jobs.

I was most struck, however, that many of the "remedies" we pursue on the Iron Range were attempted and failed in Gruchow's hometown. As Gruchow writes,

> "When we sell ourselves, in the name of economic development, as ideally suited for the least attractive kinds of factory work because our people are willing to labor hard and at subsistence wages without complaining or organizing, or when we allow the rest of society to dump its toxic trash in our land because we'll do anything for a few jobs, what are we telling our children about our ideals, our hopes and dreams?"

On the Iron Range, finding new jobs is a priority. Right now, we are billed as a place where a hard-working, skilled workforce exists, ready to labor on the behalf of a new or existing business. This may bring jobs, but what are we telling people who live here? We're saying we can't solve our own problems; we have to win ourselves a "provider" to give us the support we need. It's no different than telling your daughter to brush up on her cooking skills to win a good husband.

If you look at the businesses that do the best in Hibbing and Chisholm, you will see that people who are committed to doing business in this area started them right here. All capitalist enterprises will, at some point in their existence, have the chance to consolidate or move in exchange for cash or prestige. The only people who are going to resist that temptation are those who give a darn about the place they hang their hat.

We must never become the place where businesses mine out cheap, complacent labor, because we are not cheap or complacent. The years of labor struggles at our local mines stand as proof of that. If we slash our standards, we'll never be taken seriously as the entrepreneurial, technological epicenter we have the potential of becoming.

And, as Gruchow asks, what are we teaching our children? What are we telling the kids in the Hibbing schools (who will see one of their old school buildings close in the next couple of years) about their prospects of living and working here? If they're the smart, hard-working kids we need, they've probably figured out that we're willing to sell out for something less than we already have. No one wants to stick around to see that happen. We tell them, in a sort of veiled language, that the Twin Cities and other metro areas hold the opportunities. The best we can hope for is to glean a tiny bit of that glory for ourselves.

Gruchow came to this conclusion:

"We raise our most capable rural children from the beginning to expect that as soon as possible they will leave and that if they are at all successful, they will never return. We impose upon them, in effect, a kind of homelessness. The work of reviving rural communities will begin when we can imagine a rural future that makes a place for at least some of our best and brightest children, when they are welcome to be at home among us. Only then will we be serious about any future at all."

The "economic development" activities we take on now will indeed determine how many jobs we have in the future, along with the type, location, and pay. However, they will also declare our core values, our ideal society, and our hopes for our children.

Gruchow's words weren't written about the Iron Range, but they fit. All of us, from our leaders on down to the least involved citizen, should ask ourselves his question, "What are we teaching rural children?" The decisions we make now will answer it in years to come.

Gruchow, who suffered from severe depression, committed suicide in 2004.

Aaron and Henry

The Wisdom of Fathers

KAXE Commentary, June 2007

Allow me one cliché: Nothing in my life has compared to holding my son right after he was born. For ten minutes, Henry and I looked at each other as his mother recovered from surgery and the rest of our family drove in to meet the new arrival. I wish I could say that I told him how to tie a square knot or change the oil on a truck, but I realized right then that I didn't have those answers for him. I dropped out of Boy Scouts because of my failure to tie knots, and though I descend from five generations of Iron Range mechanics, miners, and engineers, I can barely describe what separates internal combustion from magic.

It took me a while to realize my influence as Henry's dad. When he was really little, I played a game where he would lightly slap my face and I would do an exaggerated head jerk, like you see in pro wrestling or a stage adaptation of *Gone with the Wind*. Henry would laugh, and I would laugh, and it was all so cute – until he punched a little girl three months later. He didn't mean to hurt her, and she was fine, but we had to change our game after that. It's so easy to forget how important parents are in the lives of their kids. I've heard of teenagers rejecting the teachings of their parents, something I know is coming, but I also know that no one escapes the influence of their upbringing.

My dad and I were unlike each other in most ways. Growing up, his mind hummed with animated schematics for transmissions, boat motors, and automatic weapons, while mine lit up for sentences, paragraphs, and poetry. On this Father's Day, though, I realize that we are more alike than we once thought. We both want very much to have the wisdom to explain this hard world to our sons. Dad, who was built like a leather whip, once told me that if I got in a fight with someone bigger than me, to hit first, knock the man down, and hit his head on something hard. The guy wouldn't expect it, and the best chance to avoid a beating comes in the first fifteen seconds of a fight. At the time that seemed bizarre, probably inappropriate advice to give a boy. But then I caught myself telling Henry, who is two, that Thomas the Tank Engine lives in England because Dwight Eisenhower sunk all our money in the Interstate instead of high-speed rail. "What?" I imagine Henry saying one day. My father and I are different, but our effort to make life simple to understand is no less futile. Still, we try in our own ways. That is the quest I inherit from my father.

The other night, Henry had a nightmare. He tried to tell me about it, but he can't quite talk yet, and I couldn't understand. Maybe it was a monster. Maybe he just felt alone. His arms and legs shook as I held him, and he cried for an hour and a half. Nothing would soothe him. As he finally wore out and fell asleep again, I wondered who would hold him like that when he was older? The day will come when my arms won't be big enough anymore. All I can do is pass along whatever wisdom I can, hoping that some day it will come in handy.

So remember, Henry. Your best chance to win a fight with someone bigger and meaner than you is in the first fifteen seconds. Surprise them and, please, please, just stay safe.

Amanda, Aaron, and Alyssa Brown—1984

Junkyard Phoenix

In 1988, despite the strong support of a young boy waving from the septic mound of a failing junkyard on Highway 7, Michael Dukakis's presidential hopes died. Homeless frogs also died from good intentions. A skunk died in an oil barrel. My toy government fell when my sister used key members of the Cabinet as bracelet charms.

The women in my family tell me 1988, and the years surrounding it, were among their worst. The men generally don't care to discuss it. I view those years with wonder. Though my family no longer owns the junkyard, you can still see how the spilled oil and wrecked cars marked the landscape left behind. I drive down Highway 7 when I leave the Iron Range, even when it would be faster to take the four-lane highway. I slow down, stop when there's no traffic, and look at the same green and white trailer, the road where I learned to ride my bicycle and, in the distance, I see the old workshop where my family rebuilt countless wrecks.

Dukakis was the most famous person to pass by the junkyard. My mother, father, and sisters still doubt this claim, but I know what I saw. In late summer 1988, the legendarily short, Greek, tank-riding presidential candidate appeared at a rally on northern Minnesota's Mesabi Iron Range. Most traveling north from the Twin Cities or Duluth would take the four-lane State Highway 53 a few miles over, but I suspected that the Secret Service might try an alternate route past our place for security reasons.

I was eight, but oddly knowledgeable in this area, having used an encyclopedia to appoint small toys to positions in the executive, legislative, and judicial branches of a federal government I carried around. (I recall being disappointed that so many Congressional and Supreme Court seats were held by twelve-for-a-dollar expressionless pink dinosaur erasers, but I had no idea how close to reality I had come).

A boy raised on a junkyard isn't born with an interest in government or politics. My passions stemmed from a trip to Washington, D.C. I had won from a children's invention contest the year before. Prior to that, I had never been to a city larger than Duluth. Afterward, I could say that I had stood where the president gave his State of the Union address, visited the Smithsonian, been in a cab, heard other languages, and seen a black person. That's a lot in five days. To win the contest, I had invented a set of seatbelt covers that would encourage kids to buckle up. One part of the buckle would have an image of a dog or duck; the other would have a doghouse or duck pond so kids could make a game out of putting on the seatbelt. The previous year's winner had invented a spoon that cats could eat, so I guess the judges wanted something a little more sober. The contest paid for me and one parent to go to Washington. My parents couldn't afford another ticket, but the faculty at my elementary school passed the hat. The school board had just voted to close Forbes Elementary (The building is now a country saloon, with free throw lines still on the gym floors and a big foot-pedal sink outside the restrooms). Most of the teachers would either be reassigned to another school or laid off, but somehow they raised enough money for my family to go on the trip. In the collapse of their country school, they saw in me something that could be salvaged.

After the trip, I followed the 1988 election closely and was excited for the Dukakis visit to northern Minnesota. For most, an early specter of despair hovered over Dukakis's electoral hopes that summer. After all, the Democratic presidential nominee was forced to defend a region that last went Republican for Herbert Hoover. At the same time, an unseen sense of gloom hung over the junkyard. Business was poor, and the pressures of the past, family life, and alcohol corroded my parents' marriage like rust on the vehicles piled behind our home. In all of this, I remained blissfully unaware. It was summer. Dukakis would be president. The family would have more room when we added a new trailer onto our current one to form a "T" shape. And the defending World Champion Minnesota Twins would win again this year, and next.

The day Dukakis was to speak on the Iron Range, I scribbled a crayon "Vote Dukakis" poster featuring a donkey with a cane. During that period in my artistic career, all subjects carried canes or swords. I appreciated the utilitarian aspect of giving my creations tools. I was also very bad at drawing fingers. We had peace in 1988, so I opted for cane, not sword. I asked my parents if I could hang the drawing in the window of the trailer when Dukakis came by. At the time, Dad tended to vote with the editorial board of *The Shooting Times* and lacked enthusiasm for the cane-wielding Second Amendment threat I had begat. Mom explained that Dukakis would not be passing in front of our home, nor would anyone be able to see the sign 100 feet from the road. Mom leaned left in her politics, so I still think this was more of a commentary on my donkey.

Disappointed, but not deterred, I wandered out to the front yard with my drawing. In those days, and today for that matter, I filled up the blank moments of life with stories. I wrote the script and watched amazing possibilities play out behind the Coke bottle glasses I wore. I imagined Dukakis stepping from a sleek, dark car on the roadside in his long, black coat. He shook my hand as I told him my name and pointed to the junkyard where I lived. I gave him the picture, explained the donkey's cane, and offered to introduce him to my miniature federal government. Of course, I knew he would not be able to stay long because of his speaking engagement to the north. I thought that he might remember my name one day at the White House and invite me over.

None of this happened, but a black limousine did streak down Highway 7 that afternoon. I watched it from atop the septic mound in front of our mobile home. Dukakis was probably the only non-corpse within 100 miles of that spot who might have merited such a vehicle. Still, no one believed me. "It's Dukakis," I yelled to my two younger sisters who were picking wildflowers. We were born within a three-year span, and while the girls shared my enthusiasm for seeing a limousine, to them, Dukakis could just as easily have been the name of an unpopular Care Bear. My mother also assured me it was not him, and my dad had already gone to work in the shop.

I didn't mind that no one believed me. If it wasn't him, whoever was in that limo was the most famous person to pass by Brown and Sons Salvage.

Set in rolling hills of wrecked vehicles, Brown and Sons Salvage was comprised of a cavernous workshop, attached office, two arch-style steel storage buildings, and two trailer houses: one filled with hubcaps, the other with my family. The entire junkyard hugged the inside of a big curve along County Highway 7. That curve is one of few directional variations on a long, straight path through one of the world's largest tamarack tree marshes, loosely connecting the

Proctor rail-yards and Duluth shipyards to the mines of the Iron Range. If the local iron mines churned out the stuff that made steel, then the place where I grew up was where the steel "Went to Be with its Lord," a phrase borrowed from local newspaper obituaries. Cars and trucks came in twisted on flat bed trucks and left either in parts or in heavy crushed cubes.

Brown & Sons Salvage Wrecker

My grandfather was Brown and my dad, the on-site manager, was the eldest of the Sons. Grandpa opened the junkyard after a career that included, among other things, truck driving and iron mining. My father was one of thousands of Iron Rangers laid off in the mid-eighties: most from the mines, my dad from Cummins Diesel. His childhood was marked by hard work, troubles, his parents' divorce, and the death of his mother. I never met my grandmother, but her death when my dad was in high school seemed to affect him enough that I still keep a picture of her holding my dad when he was a baby. The junkyard was a new beginning for my father and grandfather. With all the difficulty of his childhood behind him, Dad wanted to build a family stronger than the one he grew up in. He and his father shared a love of building, fixing, and tinkering, and from this, the junkyard rose from the ashes of dark years.

The junkyard ultimately proved to be an ill-fated endeavor in the employment history of my dad and grandfather. As an enterprise, it went the way of the wrecked vehicles it salvaged and sold. To me, however, it never seemed a failure. From age four to age twelve, I learned most of my vocabulary and developed my interests in a place that, by current zoning standards, would be enclosed in a fence to keep the surrounding uninhabitable swamp in good taste.

I learned a few things growing up where I did. For instance, it was a junkyard, but if you called it a salvage yard, it sounded better. Call it a salvage center, and it even sounded classy. But none of this made the place any less of a junkyard. You could mold words how you liked, but on the junkyard, everything ended up in one of two piles: stuff that worked and stuff that didn't. If it worked or could be fixed, we could sell it and make a few bucks. We made money off the stuff that didn't work, too, but it was harder. Everything on the junkyard that didn't work eventually faced the fire. Anything metal was crushed into a cube and sold to recyclers who melted it into new metal. Lesser material was burned out back. If it couldn't work, it became smoke and a memory.

I learned that the junkyard was a place for people who had no place. The junkyard clientele wasn't limited to one political ideology; however, whether Republican or Democrat, these were the people who connected the arrows on their ballots with blood. Michael Dukakis would not have blended in at the junkyard, but neither would George Bush. Not many did. In a sea of wrecked cars and vast outbuildings full of sorted parts, humans of any kind were a vocal minority among the metal and rust. The regular customers felt comfortable there but uncomfortable anywhere else. Mechanically-inclined misfits found friendly refuge among the dead vehicles.

Also finding sanctuary in our junkyard were thousands of frogs, clinging to life in an abnormal setting. My sisters and I took special interest in their welfare. The county made my family pile fifteen-foot mounds of dirt to block the view of all the wrecks, resulting in a muddy bog along the inside of these great dirt walls. Thus, an unnaturally large population of frogs settled in the muck. I can still picture a ball of tadpoles clinging to life in an evaporating July puddle. Sometimes we'd leave the hose running to save them, but in a dry year even that could only delay their demise. With so many frogs around, my sisters and I provided accommodations for some, especially those down on their luck. The artificial frog pond by the Great Wall of Dirt occasionally dried out completely and at other times, a thin layer of oil ran off from the junkyard and covered the brown water. When the frog refugees poured out of the pond, we'd keep as many as we could grab in a plastic toddler swimming pool outside the back door of the trailer. One year, the frost came early, and we found about a half dozen frogs floating motionless underneath a thin sheet of ice in the pool. We decided that the frogs needed to be warmed, and warmed fast. In a clear piece of my mom's Tupperware, we drew water about as hot as one would like a winter bath and dropped in the frogs. At that moment, three things occurred: the frogs – in shock from the temperature change – sprung to life and vomited most of their internal organs, my father entered the kitchen to start the morning coffee, and everyone involved (except the frogs) screamed. We learned the difference between cold and warm-blooded animals that day and that a frog's place was outside. It didn't seem fair. The home our junkyard had carelessly created for them was so unstable. I imagine some frogs made it to better places, but the driveway was littered with those who didn't.

On the junkyard, I learned that oil, dirt, and darkness meant hard work, not something to fear, but also not something easy to understand. Every night, my mom and dad would read my sisters and I a story of our choosing and kiss each of us on the forehead before bed. One night, Dad was working late, removing an engine from a Mack truck with his brothers and my grandfather. I really didn't want to skip the ritual that night, so Mom drove us back to the shop to cash in on our nighttime sendoff. We opened the workshop door and saw unfamiliar men perched atop ladders, working on a metal monster suspended from the ceiling over the truck. Their faces, arms, and clothing were black with grease. My mom told one of the men why we were there, and he jumped from the ladder. As he walked toward me, I recognized my father and was relieved. He bent down and kissed me on the forehead. The other men smiled with white teeth, and then I recognized my uncles. I did not notice, nor would I have cared, about the beer cans lying around, but my mother did. Despite the cold drafts attacking my thin summer pajamas, I felt warm.

Salvage operations generally succeed by focusing on volume. If you deal in late model wrecks, mechanics and resellers will buy in bulk. Junkyards fail when they load up on older vehicles, where lack of demand and rust cuts into the sum of their parts' value. Unfortunately, my family learned this the hard way. Our junkyard had the reputation of being the place to find older parts you couldn't find elsewhere, but we never sold many parts. My family spent most of the junkyard years knowing that it probably wouldn't work out in the long run.

I don't know if it was a moment of realization, or just the dull ache that you eventually learn is arthritis. Voters had a moment of realization when they saw my man Dukakis riding around in an Army tank later that year. He wore an oversized helmet, and he generally looked out of place, like a frog who realized that his bog was slowly filling with oil, but who needed the bog's ten electoral votes. Almost twenty years later (and probably for the next half century) "Dukakis in the tank" is a public relations term for a photo opportunity that accomplishes the exact opposite of its intended purpose. He took a huge hit in the political tracking polls, which I followed with the same vigor as the status of the frogs.

That same summer, my dad got a call one evening from my uncle who was working in the shop. A skunk had crawled atop a used oil barrel and slipped inside and couldn't get out. It was hissing and growling inside the barrel. The evenings still stayed light until late, and the sky had just turned orange beyond the railroad tracks on the other side of the junkyard. Dad wrestled a gun out of his bedroom closet. Since we had taken such effort to rescue local frogs, the execution of a wayward skunk didn't sit well with us kids. My mother protested as well. Shooting the skunk would only ensure that it stinks up the whole area, she said. I didn't hear my father's final logic for walking back to the oil barrel with his gun. Accounts of the proceedings vary. I just know that after a few minutes we heard a gunshot, and a few moments later (and for the next week) the house, the yard, and my dad smelled like a dead skunk. Years later, I thought how the skunk and Dukakis faced similar challenges – one in an inescapable oil barrel with ill-willed humans circling around it, Dukakis in a tank, probably feeling out of place knowing that he's only there to boost the military credibility of a New England governor who, given the choice between cane and sword, would probably select cane. Neither skunk nor Dukakis '88 would rise from the rubble that year, but I hold their memories.

A boy who follows politics at eight does not become a mechanic or truck driver. A boy who goes to college and attains privilege unknown in his childhood never feels comfortable among privilege. There is pride and shame in growing up on a junkyard. Through ingenuity, you can build something new in life, something that works, but it will never be like the new car fresh off the lot with that special smell.

A new car runs smoothly, but on the junkyard, you learn that it is only a number of years that separate the new models you see on

TV from the scrap heap. This fact crushes some people, but not my family. So long as the steel is sound, new life can be found. Missed expectations and hardship marked my dad's childhood. His parents' marriage rattled apart, but he and my mom succeeded in keeping our childhoods reasonably happy, even though their own marriage later rattled apart, too. From this, I found what worked, and I began the life-long search for what I can't yet understand. In this, I have met some success, but also some failure. That is the nature of my family's work. From my failures, too, something can be salvaged.

Someone once asked me if I was ever bothered that the cars hauled into the junkyard might have just recently been in a fatal accident, some perhaps with dark red evidence of the terrible crash stained deep in the upholstery. As a kid, I never thought about it. Now, I hold a practical view. Once you remove the dead relatives, a salvageable transmission might remain in that splayed out Ford. Are you really going to bury that transmission? Will you mourn it? If it works, it can be salvaged. True for cars. True for people. More than one marriage in my family tragically crossed the center line. No parent/child relationship or business endeavor ever managed to avoid pain or crisis. Casualties mounted and many cars never drove again. That's how it is on the junkyard. We found value in the surviving parts.

I have three young sons now, Henry, Doug, and George. They look a lot like I did when I was younger. In a strange way, I'm disappointed that the backgrounds of their childhood pictures will not feature cars twisted beyond recognition. Despite, or perhaps because of the wrecked relationships and business ventures of my family's past, my life has already been easier than my father's or grandfather's. As I hold my boys, I hope I can teach them what I have learned. I will show them how to help the frogs. I will show them to find worth in causes that seem lost. I will show them that people and relationships can be salvaged, just like car parts. They can be better, if they want to be. If my life story should burst into flames through fault or fate, my only hope is that my boys will rise from the embers. It is the unifying hope of every generation of my family. We are a people of oily feathers and majestic beaks of scarred steel. We are the junkyard phoenix. As surely as I will one day be smoke and a memory, I believe in the hope that something good can rise from my ashes.

Our ashes.

The Daddy War

Today's television viewers and web surfers know the constant cultural tug of war presented as the modern struggle between work and family. Without it, the *Today Show, Good Morning America,* and the like would be forced to cover the news, sending people scurrying away from the television like zombies for brains. It doesn't matter whether you're a man or woman, married or single; if you have kids and a job you are doing something that will probably ruin, A) your children's future; or B) the American economy; or even C) all of that, and God hates you, according to someone somewhere who recently got a lucrative book deal. I'm on the front lines of this battle, which feels less like a battle and more like a sticky, loud stalemate involving people wearing diapers. It doesn't help that my daddy issues put me out of step with the local custom.

The Iron Range is a highly traditional place. Though people come from many different ethnic backgrounds, the central idea of parenting in our blue collar world was, until very recently, universal. Dad worked, sometimes underground, usually somewhere dirty, and brought home the dirt and the money which mom cleaned up and spent, respectively. Dad ran the show, sometimes literally, but usually figuratively, the way the British monarch is technically still in charge of Canada. Mom took care of the house, but even in the old days, it was common for Iron Range moms to take a part or full time job to make ends meet. Dad would go hunting and fishing for days at a time, and mom would send the kids outside, regardless of season or weather, so she could enjoy peace. In any event, there was a system that was not necessarily fair, but clear. Labor division was based on gender roles. Dad shot encroaching bears and changed the oil in the car. Mom cooked the meals and buried her resentment. Kids would figure out their colors and develop their cognitive whatnot when they went to school. That's what schools were for.

While this remains true in pockets of the country, including large portions of the Iron Range, cultural changes have upended this system elsewhere. That's not news to most people, but it is to some I've met. I have a job that allows me flex time to work from home. Additionally, I am a college teacher, which means my work time fluctuates greatly in a calendar year. Sometimes I'm very busy, and sometimes, I get to watch cartoons with the kids at ten a.m. while eating Goldfish crackers. With the exception of my meetings, classes, and office hours, I don't necessarily have to be anywhere at any particular time.

On the other hand, my wife and I have adopted what might be the "new typical" approach to parenting our three boys. There's a little of the old tradition in that Christina stays home to manage the household, working only occasionally to bring in extra money. But we use the team approach to parenting, both changing diapers, handling chores and finances, running errands, feeding kids, etc. At prescribed times I do my work, which for me, involves firing up my laptop computer and teaching online, writing, or blogging. But it is nothing like the picture of "daddy going to work" that most Iron Rangers carry around in their memories. There's no "wait 'til your father gets home," because quite often, I already am. Where I once looked up to my dad overhauling a truck engine, my sons see me at the computer grading papers, answering e-mail, or blogging about the latest outrage in Iron Range economic development policy. When visiting neighbors or contractors see me working, they assume that I am unemployed or disabled in a way that you can't see on the outside. Sometimes I think people would rather I were unemployed, because that's something that folks who work in the mines or in the trades understand.

One time, the carpenter who built our house was doing some finishing work while I was working at the dining room table. It just so happened, and I'm not proud of this, that I was still wearing ratty sweats, a t-shirt, and my biologically living bathrobe (my "morningwear"). Our high-strung cairn terrier Molly bolted out the gate while John was working on something outside, so he and I chased her down our dirt road. When she veered into the woods, I pursued, thankful I had decided to leave my slippers on that morning. I caught her, picked her up, and the three of us walked back to the house. When we arrived by the spot where John was working, he said, "Well, back to work." I said, "Yup, me too." There was a moment, me in my bathrobe with an insane canine tucked beneath my arm, where I noticed a chasm between my work and the traditional work the Iron Range is known for. And it's only become more complicated as I explain my work to my kids, who, probably through genetics, have shown far more interest in toy dump trucks and backhoes than in daddy's boring news shows.

The real clash occurs along the margins of this system. When is work time and when is play time? What's the difference? How do you navigate the day when your hobby and work are interrelated and your family might surround you the entire time? And dammit, why does the Internet have to have so much cool stuff to look at instead of working? This is my struggle, the struggle of a modern dad. And while it may not be the same struggle that faced the broad shouldered fathers of Iron Range history, I share with them a credo: I just want to work hard so my kids have it better. That said, I would understand if my kids sought employment that did not include bathrobes and laptops. I still can't shake my doubts about that myself.

A World of Work

In a thousand ways, the Iron Range functions at an economic disadvantage to other areas of the country. We're ninety miles away from a major port. We're north of the major east-west trade routes. Our main product – iron ore used to make steel – is essential to the economy, but we're still waiting to be trusted with the means to produce steel here ourselves. In the 1950s, the most accessible stores of pure iron ore ran out, leaving only the complicated practice of processing lower grade iron taconite for use in steelmaking. Miners blast taconite out of the earth into great boulders, crush it, heat it up to 1,290 degrees to bond it with other elements, and ship it off to a place where the stone cold pellets are heated up again, even hotter, to make steel. Out-of-state and international companies own all of our ore operations, and more than ever, the success of the steel industry depends on tiny margins in the expense ledger. If profits dip even an eyelash below the straight black line, somebody, probably everybody, on the Range will get the shaft.

So why does the Iron Range still exist?

The answer depends on who you talk to. Some would say the area's political and business sectors have rescued us with economic development efforts. Practically, our region remains a reliable source of raw materials and still has an effective industrial labor force, even if that labor is more expensive than in other parts of the world. So long as the United States remains more stable than other parts of the world, it behooves the nation to keep our domestic steel production going.

But the real reason we're still here is because the Iron Range is a working place. Since the start of the industrial era, the Iron Range has endured boom and bust economies, attracting people who would rather endure such economic shifts than live in a big city or chase work elsewhere. When times are bad, people here find ways to survive. In the 20th century, that usually meant logging or farming when the mines were down. Only about ten percent of the current Range population works directly in the mining industry, so things have changed some. Still, it's a boom and bust place where mining still anchors our economy. Most folks committed to living here long term know that they may have to dig up some other way of life if their current gig runs out, as most gigs eventually do. That creates resourcefulness and a strong work ethic. I've seen many examples of dedicated Iron Rangers losing one job only to open a small business, go back to school, or catch on someplace else even when abandoning the area would be an easy option.

So far, I've been fortunate enough to maintain control over my job situations, though I've already switched careers a couple times. During the two years I was editor of the *Hibbing Daily Tribune*, I received invitations to cover or attend economic development meetings, where discussions often turned to Iron Range "work ethic" as a means to attract new development.

Journalism is the craft of explaining things briefly and accurately. There are no two words in the English language that do more to confound this mission than the multi-syllabic duo "economic development." What is economic development? How can it be explained briefly? Just what constitutes accuracy in explaining a process where hundreds of thousands of public and private dollars transfer electronically to different accounts with the goal of attracting an Applebee's restaurant on the edge of town? A town, I might add, where a third of the population still resents the construction of four-lane freeways and another third are blood relatives or drinking buddies with the economic development consultant pulling the strings. Try wrapping that into a thirty-word sentence with an active verb.

That leaders and power brokers place so much emphasis on economic development efforts on the Iron Range shows how much things have changed since the first developers came here. Early prospectors were motivated only by the feverish demand for ore and timber that existed at the time. They didn't need any extra incentives to develop because the financial benefit of harvesting wood and mining ore was incentive enough. Now technology, the economy, and work itself have changed so much that it's extremely difficult to attract the same kinds of developers that lined up to hire Iron Rangers in the early 1900s.

Let's go back to the work ethic argument heard so often at the meetings I attended. This argument, that Rangers just plain work harder, makes a lot of anecdotal sense. Immigrants came here for work, not pleasure. Many of the fastest growing parts of the country today exist because people are looking for pleasure. Suburbs are "nicer" than inner cities or small towns, so people move there. Money follows them and development explodes. The Iron Range was never especially "nice." Sure we have trees, lakes, and pretty nature, but so do hundreds of other places within driving distance. People came here from all over the world to work. The money from the work went to bring more family here and establish a new life, but hard work was the cornerstone. That attitude passed from one generation to another.

Lazy is just not an option for most people on the Iron Range. In the Range crowds I've run in, the word "lazy" is a greater insult than "fat, stupid, shithead." I worked my way through high school and college, at times putting in fulltime hours on top of an overloaded school schedule. Part of this is just me. Professional achievement has always been my barometer of personal success. But part of it, I think, comes from this local attitude that work comes first, an attitude that has existed on the Iron Range for many generations.

Most of my dad's stories about his childhood have to do with work. Family turmoil marked his teen years. He and his brothers moved a lot and spent countless hours with my grandfather on an endless list of tasks. Dad lost count of how many sand point wells they dug. He told me once that he wanted my sisters and I to have an easier time growing up than he had. Dad and I dug just one sand point well when I was a kid, and the ease of my childhood showed because I really wasn't much use to him. If you've never dug a sand point well by hand, here's how it works. You thread a pointed pipe into the ground in a spot where you think there might be water. My dad used one of those crazy divining rods made out of a clothes hanger to find a spot. I thought this was insane until fifteen years later when I saw a professional well driller use the same stupid thing to find a spot for a well at my house. Once your first pipe is in, you either use sledge hammers or a post driver to pound the pipe into the ground, adding lengths of pipe as you go. The well we dug for my dad's garage took three days of work to get deep enough to draw water. My dad said many of the wells he had to dig as a kid never found water and had to be dug again in a new spot. Believe me, this experience gave me new perspective on the idea of work.

Because my dad allowed me to avoid the labor camp atmosphere he remembered, I was able to define work in my own way. For me, work usually involves paper. As a kid, my preferred work was to read as much as possible and write things that would either earn me good grades or make the other kids laugh with me instead of at me. My first humor column was written on a piece of notebook paper and passed around class. It might have been about boogers, or maybe having to go to the bathroom. With one exception, all of my jobs have involved paper, the media, or the Internet.

The exception, my first job, was when I delivered pizzas at age sixteen. For the mechanically inclined men of my family, who in my mind will always be doing "real" work as I frolic at a keyboard, pizza delivery is a pretty lame example of physical labor. I worked at a joint that could never decide if it was a pizza place with a bar downstairs or a bar with a pizza place upstairs. After answering a classified ad, my interview took place on a bar stool. It was three p.m., and my would-be boss was of the belief that the drinking day starts at noon, not five. He looked at me and asked only one question. "Do you have a car, a license, and insurance?" Yes, I said, reaching for my wallet that had the cards. "Nah," he said, drinking beer with one hand and waving the other indifferently. "I believe you."

In a quirky humor novel, that would be considered literary foreshadowing.

That summer I cooked my share of pizzas and lowered many a chicken appendage into the fryer; the fryer job paid the least and was the most "work" of any job I've had since. Delivering pizzas can tell you more about a town than any census. Walk around a mall or park and you'll see part of a town. You have to knock on doors while carrying food to see the rest of the town. For a writer, this sort of thing can't be learned at a college.

One time, during my last two weeks as a delivery driver, I brought a pizza to the tiny upstairs apartment of a triplex. The ceiling slanted, and the door was just wide enough to accommodate a pizza box. Living there was a tall black man with an afro haircut who had to duck to talk to me. Also there: his girlfriend and a few hundred baby birds. My concern for speedy deliveries had waned since giving my two-weeks notice, so I accepted his invitation to show me how he fed his birds with a tiny eye-dropper. From the sheer number of birds, I imagine that's what he did all day long. I wonder if he thought of it as work.

If anything, delivering pizza taught me that my childhood tendency to seek out paper instead of hard labor was probably a sign of my destiny. At my second job, I was an overnight disk jockey at WEVE in Eveleth, an AM/FM station that played adult contemporary music. Even with all the Michael Bolton and Paula Abdul, it was a pretty cool gig for a high school kid. But all entry level jobs have their eccentricities. I worked alone in the station at night. In the winter, my responsibilities included running through waist-deep snow outside the station to clear snow and ice out of a large dish to maintain a satellite feed. A stick hung above the studio wall for the express purpose of whacking the dish until the snow fell out. Posted next to the control board was a list of songs long enough to facilitate dish whacking (My favorite was "American Pie" at a comfortable eight minutes, twenty-eight seconds). In the summer, however, the most physically taxing thing I did on a shift was walk over to the deck that abutted the second-floor studio to smoke cigarettes while watching cars pass on Highway 53.

In my third job, working as a worksite inspector for a youth job training program, I actually sat in a cubicle on the days I wasn't out on the road. My job was to write reports and press releases. Though I spent a lot of days in the car visiting worksites, I was only gathering information for said reports and press releases. My first two jobs – pizza guy and overnight disc jockey – were full of odd, colorful anecdotes. In this new job, I sat at a computer, staring at motivational posters that featured eagles and vibrant corporate buzzwords like "Clarity" and "Excellence." I observed nine a.m. and three p.m. coffee breaks, learning the speech patterns of my office mates: "Hey, big shooter," "Howdy ho," and "Let me tell you, in great detail, about my cat."

In any event, I was so deskbound in my work, that I found myself walking to get a drink of water only to ensure that a deadly blood clot would not form in my leg. Even on the days out of the office, my actual work involved driving a car, which in modern terms, is no more physical than a day *in* the office. It continued this way every workday for three summers as I saved up to pay for college. Then, one day, I was given new orders. I was to supervise a group of high school students who had some hours to make up for the work program. We were to meet out in the woods somewhere about thirty miles north of Virginia, where our office was, and plant pine seedlings on a logging site. Wearing the same khaki pants and polo shirt combo I wore most days, I donned work boots and gloves and, for a glorious day in the sun, planted trees down a long row. Those trees are probably still there today, and in about a decade or two they'll mature enough to be harvested. In all likelihood, they will become paper. That's right, paper. The lifeblood of my whole existence. In almost all ways, the worksite inspector gig was a great job for a college student, full of experience and opportunity. But on the one day I planted trees, I had caused a course of action that would provide all the paper I – a writer and teacher – would use in my entire lifetime. Now *that* is a good day's work.

This illustrates one of the biggest changes that I and other Iron Rangers of my generation have to face. The work we do now is, on average, quite different from the work of our parents and grandparents. Physically, much of what we do is easier now, but it requires more training. These days, I mostly sit at a desk and occasionally stand in front of a classroom. The heaviest thing I lift is my bag of books and files. Compare that to the time when people my age from my kind of family would spend a day stripping raw ore out of an underground mine shaft. I "do" plenty. I write columns, essays, reports, grant proposals, presentations, lessons, and assignments. I build web sites. I design ads, brochures, and posters. I blog. But if I were to wear one of those tracking devices like scientists pin to bears, it would appear as though I hadn't moved at all in the course of a work day. If I really was a bear in a study, some grim scientist looking at a magnetic board would probably slide my name from "live bear" to "dead bear."

The Iron Range has always been a place for hard working people, but how will that hold up in an era when, for most, work means uploading and downloading, not picking and shoveling? The Iron Range always made room for engineers and politicians, accountants and lawyers. But will it be able to make room for web designers, software engineers, inventors, and, for that matter, job titles that don't even exist yet? Because if the answer is a sincere "yes," the Range will also have to accept change. That has never been our strong suit.

I teach at a community college. Culturally speaking, this is a relatively acceptable career choice on the Iron Range. However, about half of my teaching load is online, which means that those classes don't meet in person. Our work is done through message boards, written journals, and e-mail. This is not especially earth-shattering for anyone who follows higher education, but to explain this to many of my family members and folks I meet around town, you would think I was working on a mind-reading helmet. "You mean the class is *inside* the computer?"

The Range is not alone in this problem. Look at Detroit. Look at Columbus. Look at port cities and farming towns. Any place that once rewarded workers for putting their back into their work for eight hours or more, is now dealing with the fact that brains are more important. And American brains are expensive, so you better have a real good reason we shouldn't farm out the job to Asia. Yes, the titans of our economy still prize a good work ethic: the desire to do the job right, with pride, and teach your children the same.

But such qualities are only marginally useful to them without innovation and critical thinking. The old cliché, work smarter not harder, is only half right. A place like the Iron Range, even with its grand history, must work smarter and harder.

Why do we still exist? I think we exist because we were taught that good people work hard. We exist because we later learned that resourcefulness and hard work will keep our houses warm and our vehicles running. We exist because we say so. Change is coming, and if we want to remain in existence, we will need to say so again in new ways.

What a Guy Ought to do

KAXE Commentary, October 2007

Country life requires connections. Sure, city people say "networking" is the key to success, and that might be true. The stakes are just plain higher out in the vast, wooded, wilderness surrounding the Mesabi Iron Range. Who do you call when a big tree falls on your road or when your septic system needs to be pumped? You better have an answer, or you won't be able to go to work or use flush toilets.

First things first, you have to know the language. The exact phrase differs based on your location and ethnic background, but pay attention any time you hear some variation of the words, "What a guy ought to do" from a northern Minnesotan. This means you're going to get important advice from someone knowledgeable, worded passively to avoid acting like a big shot. And please don't be offended if the word "guys" is used interchangeably for women as well as men. This is necessary from a linguistic standpoint because the phrase "What a gal ought to do" usually precedes some form of sexual harassment.

If you're new to northern Minnesota, you need to understand the unchanging nature of our proper nouns. For instance, you might ask your neighbor where to find a good daycare center. They might say, "Oh, there's one in the old Super One." Of course, they don't mean the large building with the giant sign identifying it as the Super One grocery store. They mean the old Super One, now home to several government agencies and, yes, a daycare center. How about liquor? You can get all the liquor you need at the old Kentucky Fried Chicken. No, not the current KFC. That place is still dry, even if it is greasy. I mean the steeple-topped former KFC that is now a liquor store. It can all be pretty confusing.

The philosophy of "what a guy ought to do" is sacred in northern Minnesota. The economy has always depended on volatile natural resource industries, which means we ride a roller coaster from "OK" times to "times that could be a little better." People here always respond during the rough patches by helping each other and becoming more self-reliant. Thus our woods run thick with jacks-of-all-trades who never advertise. These are the people who can sell you a modified chainsaw and tell you how to use it. They will take your aluminum cans and give you their knowledge. You should listen to them. Sometimes, advice may sound like this:

"What a guy ought to do is go up the Scenic Highway past the old Iron Range community hall and turn left down the thin dirt access path that leads into the forest. It's behind the old gas station where they had those ice cream cones. No, not that one. The old one. Follow the path for three-quarters of a mile and build a raft from the branches of that dying birch tree by the river where they found Stinky Sipola dead in his boat. His old boat; his kid had the new one on Rainy Lake that weekend. Go down river seven miles and land underneath the railroad trestle. A guy named Shaky lives in a hollowed oak back there, and he can fix your lawnmower. He's reasonable, and I don't go to anyone else. Tell him I sent you. He doesn't like strangers. Just ask Stinky Sipola."

Of course, you're under no obligation to follow advice like that. But if you do, you'll be one step closer to understanding life in these North Woods. What a guy ought to do is keep an open mind.

Portable Screen Gazebo
Loses Luster in High Winds

Hibbing Daily Tribune, July 2002

Sunny skies. A scrumptious lunch. A view of the lake. That sounds nice, doesn't it? Nothing can go wrong with that situation. It's a great way to spend a hot summer afternoon on your day off.

That's the idea Christina and I had.

We had planned to take a picnic lunch out to the lake, go swimming, and perhaps read comfortably in a screen tent borrowed from the in-laws.

Let the good times roll.

Only one problem. No matter how sunny the day or how intricate the plans, something is always waiting in the weeds to muck it up. In our case, that something was deer flies and gale force winds.

We left the bustling metropolis of Hibbing shortly before lunchtime, heading out to the family spread somewhere out in the boonies (Lake Boony, if you're curious). We arrived, turned off the air-conditioned car, and listened intently to the cool air making a snappy noise as it turned into air about as hot as jet exhaust.

Opening the door, I was welcomed by a deer fly the size of a Cessna.

Nothing to worry about – it's just one bug. It's probably just looking for a cool place to hang out. Well, it had a few thousand buddies waiting for people snacks. If I had kept still for a couple minutes, I would have had a bug beard. That's great for winning second place on *America's Funniest Home Videos*, but not the goal of a relaxing summer picnic.

That's OK, we said. That's why we brought the portable screened gazebo. Yes, that's right. Portable screened gazebo. I say that twice because I enjoy saying "gazebo."

Gazebo.

No bugs may penetrate the versatile screen of our borrowed portable gazebo. In that regard it is the Cadillac of portable screened gazebos. The only problem was that with thirty mile per hour winds tracking off Lake Boony, it would have been easier to assemble a Cadillac on the beach than that infernal portable screened gazebo.

ATTENTION GAZEBO ENGINEERS: Your concept is good. I like it. The screen keeps out bugs, the roof keeps out sun, and the six-foot zippered entry points provide easy access from both fore and aft quarters of the gazebo. Your fatal flaw is in requiring that the dome portion of the gazebo be assembled and then held aloft as the support structure is finished. Have you noticed the resemblance between the gazebo dome and a sail of an ancient Viking ship? I have. If it were not for a well-placed tree, my wife and I would have discovered Newfoundland and sacked London by Monday morning.

Bottom line, the gazebo doesn't assemble well in high winds. It doesn't assemble well when you've got a bug beard. It doesn't assemble well when the directions are really a Japanese romance novel translated into binary code.

I don't have the directions in front of me as I write this, but based on memory they said something like, "1) Connect parts to other parts to assemble gazebo. 2) Enjoy gazebo. 3) Do not attempt to burn gazebo." It is no coincidence that the directions specifically prohibit burning the gazebo because that is precisely the desire you have upon handling the gazebo.

Me: OK, what's the first step?

Directions: Attach "4" poles to "hub."

Me: OK. (Attach, attach, attach)

Directions: Next, before doing that, run poles through tent sleeve and then attach to hub.

Me: Grrr. (detach, attach, detach, attach, detach, attach)

Directions: Now attach "3" poles to "4" poles.

Me: (attach)

Directions: Just kidding! Do not burn gazebo.

Me: GRRRR!

Wind: WOOOOOOOOOO!

Bugs: Bzzzzzzzz!

Christina: (In car eating picnic lunch).

We ended up enjoying our lunch in the car and heading back to her parents' house to return the portable screen gazebo that, to this day, does not realize how close its "flame retardant" features came to their greatest challenge ever. Perhaps we will set it up again on a calmer day when I am not sporting a "bug beard" and the temperature is within the optimal gazebo operation range.

Until then, Gazebo, our picnics will be held without the benefit of your company.

Local Radar Ball:
A Source of Mystery and Intrigue

Hibbing Daily Tribune, March 2004

Before I die, I would like to see the inside of the Nashwauk radar ball.

If you ever drive Highway 65 north of Nashwauk (or as the locals call it: "Northof- nashwauk"), you know what I'm talking about. It's a giant white dome perched atop a five-story tower just a few feet from the road. Some call it "Paul Bunyan's golf ball."

I'm told the radar ball has something to do with air traffic control, or perhaps, nuclear missiles. Either way, the rotund white orb intrigues me to no end.

A couple years ago, I called the radar ball to see if I could do a story. I wanted to find out what they do in the radar ball, and maybe, just maybe, get my picture taken with some fancy equipment, such as lasers.

At the time, the local radar ball authorities said that the 9/11 attacks had changed protocol for radar ball visits. They referred me to a very perky government official who gleefully told me how the tallest non-broadcast structure within fifty miles of Nashwauk, Minn., was actually a big secret. News coverage of the gargantuan sphere could draw dangerous attention to it.

Thus, my dream of gazing upon the interior workings of the Nashwauk radar ball lingers unfulfilled. Evildoers ruined the experience for everyone, except, of course, the radar ball people, who I can only assume live in the giant pod, sleeping in tiny upright compartments and eating freeze-dried government cheese.

So here's my official plea to our government:

Hello, Government. How are you? Might I say, your large, bloated bureaucracy is looking especially lovely today. Have you had work done on it? Either way, you look like a trillion dollars, maybe more. Say, listen, about that "no visitors" policy at the Nashwauk radar ball. Yes, Nashwauk – that's about ninety miles north of Duluth. No, it's about 150 miles south of the Canadian border – in Minnesota. Yes, that's a state. Anyway, I'd like you to reconsider your policy about the radar ball. Let me tell you why.

If you don't let me look at the inside of the Nashwauk radar ball, the terrorists win. That's right. Osama bin Laden dances for joy because law-abiding Americans may no longer experience controlled visits to secure radar ball facilities in rural Midwestern mining communities.

I bet you think I'll spill the beans about what's in the radar ball. You're worried I'll tell the North Koreans or some anarchist fringe group about all the cool stuff you have in the radar ball.

That's where you would be wrong.

I am totally willing to participate in your vast government conspiracy to conceal the contents of the Nashwauk radar ball. Storage facility? Yeah, I'll tell people that's what I saw. I'll even wear a blindfold if you just let me push some buttons or peek at a radar screen. Oh, I'm sorry. Did I say "radar screen?" I meant to say "harmless video game monitor."

See what I mean? I can play ball. I'll do what it takes to see the belly of the Nashwauk radar ball.

Perhaps if people knew more about the radar ball, it would not be feared and questioned the way it is now. The delicate secrets of this shining sphere could unlock the gates to world peace. Maybe.

Brown

If not, it wouldn't hurt world peace. And I could sleep better at night.

I'll be waiting for your response, Government. You know where to find me.

Ironic Roadside Fish
Prompts Thought

Hibbing Daily Tribune, October 2004

I love irony. I love irony so much that I applied for membership in the American Irony Association, but they wouldn't let me in.

That's how much I love irony.

On the way home from a recent Twin Cities trip, I noticed an ironic billboard along I-35. Like many signs along I-35, this billboard featured a giant cartoon fish.

You have to remember that the I-35 billboards primarily target metro-area commuters and tourists. Their mental image of Northern Minnesota would not be complete without a giant cartoon fish capable of smiling. In fact, our area legislators might have better luck next session if all their proposed bills featured a supplemental cartoon fish. The fish could act out the proposal; one fish adequately funds rural schools, while another constructs an iron nugget plant.

But I digress. The giant smiling cartoon fish of which I speak was pleasant enough. The fish, wearing a classic angler's hat full of tackle, sat in a lawn chair dangling a fishing line into a lake.

Now, I understand not everything in advertising is real. Thus, I am willing to accept, temporarily, that the fish could not only survive outside water, but enjoy the experience. I'm also aware that big fish do eat small fish – so the fishing action in this billboard was plausible.

What unsettled me was that both things occurred at once. The fish, bestowed the rare gift of life on land, chose to spend it next to a lake fishing for the same food it always eats, only this time using expensive equipment.

If I'm a fish and get to breathe air for a while, I'm thinking I don't want any more uncooked crappie. I could go for some chicken. Or maybe a steak. Heck, if I'm a land-walking fish, why not flop over to the supermarket and buy me some Saltines. Who's going to say no? God?

Perhaps I read too much from the fish billboard. Some dim marketing type probably said, "People love them cartoon fish ... OOO! Let's have him fishing! That'd catch some eyeballs!" And that was probably the end of it.

The cartoon fish fits with the style I've noticed in big city competitive marketing. A radio ad here on the Iron Range might consist of a jaunty tune with a happy announcer telling us about an upcoming spaghetti feed. A Range billboard sports the name of a car dealer and text so small you probably couldn't read even if you were on the scaffolding, but you'll buy your car there anyway.

In comparison, billboards and radio ads in the Twin Cities bellow and smash into each other like bull walruses. A cartoon fish is not good enough on its own; it must also fish, smile, and wear a funny hat.

Most metro radio listening is done in cars, so advertisers must overcome sirens, signals, and traffic. Additionally, in light of Big Government's efforts to encourage liberal hippie car pools, some listeners might actually attempt human interaction during their commute. Advertisers have to do SOMETHING to put down this threat.

The result is a veritable scorched airwaves policy in which blaring bass thumps while screeching announcers shout down invisible helicopters in thirty-second rotations. Meantime billboards blare the virtues of competing TV news teams, each prettier and more serious than the last. You won't find much logic, and only those not yet desensitized by the sensory din notice the irony inherent in the cartoon fish.

Go free, cartoon fish. Live free in the North Country.

Animatronic Miners:
The Next Step?

Hibbing Daily Tribune, March 2005

Every once in awhile, it's nice to see *someone else* invest obscene sums of money into animatronic displays at historic mines that once employed actual people.

Officials are preparing a former coal mine in Lynch, Kentucky, to become a tourism hotbed, complete with robot miners, according to an AP story by Roger Alford.

The story made note of the historical significance of the coal mines in this particular town. Naturally, I can appreciate that. I'm a card-carrying member of the Hibbing Historical Society and hold great interest in our unique Iron Range history, much of it related to iron mining. However, I had to cringe when I saw that many of the Kentucky locals quoted in the story believed that the multi-million dollar coal funhouse would "rescue" their struggling town from the depths of economic duress.

I think I've seen this movie. I remember having a problem with the ending.

Here in Minnesota's Iron Range region we've learned a few things. First, our unique history deserves attention and preservation. Second, though this is a noble endeavor, it will make us, after expenses and sinkhole setbacks, exactly zero dollars.

Our tourism dollars come from fishing, hunting, and the great outdoors. Here in Hibbing, we are best served to use our connections with the arts and athletics to bring people to town. But never forget, though our history is important, people will only pay so much to see robot miners. I think the Kentucky folks will learn this when the Portal 31 mine exhibit opens sometime next year.

The Portal 31 exhibit makes copious references to the animatronic miners in its official materials, as well as in media coverage of the project. If we've learned anything from the *Terminator* movie series, it is that we should remain wary of robots forced into a robo-life of robo-labor. Just like poor people, eventually these man-bots will push back and cause trouble.

What if, tomorrow, a Kentucky scientist from the future transported back in time to the present to warn his or her ancestors of the dangers of this new endeavor?

Kentucky scientist of the future: "Your first mistake was giving the automaton a pickax. In 2009 the mine-bots learned that the plastic shields protecting the touring cars split like pudding skin under the slash of their mighty scythes." (Followed by dramatic opening strains from "Dueling Banjos").

Modern Kentucky resident: "Say, that is a purdy silver jumpsuit, hoss!" (Responds with echo chords from "Dueling Banjos")

Getting back to subject, the Portal 31 interpretive project in Lynch, Ky., is on track with several large public grants ranging from $500,000 to $1.2 million and some high hopes from local community leaders. I wish them well.

Meantime, I would advise local tourism officials to keep their eyes peeled on e-bay for some low-cost, Kentucky-based animatronic miners sometime a year or two from now. Perhaps with lower overhead, we can make the concept work here on the Iron Range.

Live and learn.

From Pine Trees to Brooms:
The Present History of the Iron Range

Part Two
In the Beginning

As the earth formed, a searing mass of lava and steam enveloped the surface, spitting out heat and forming elements, according to Marvin Lamppa's *Iron Country* (my main source for historical research in this book). That one big bubble of lava popped up just as the planet began to cool, and it was frozen in place as granite. This enormous formation represented a large divide in what we would later call the continent of North America. Enormous mountain ranges formed along the divide, on the place now called the Iron Range. These mountain ranges were bigger than anything the continent has now and overlooked a landscape that I can imagine included scaly dino-bears and flying mooseoraptors. Erosion wore down these mountains, and water bodies formed and retreated, leaving sand and other debris over the rich iron deposits that gave the place its current name. The formation of the iron deposits took at least a billion years, but the shape of our land is even older than that. The name Mesaba is a Dakota word for giant, or "Big Man Hills." Just imagine a tribal scout or traveling party coming from the north or west to see the hard ridge of the Iron Range poking up over a landscape of enormous pine trees, blocking the horizon like a massive man lying on a bed of timber. Every human who has ever lived on the Iron Range has drawn breath in the shadow of the sleeping giant, who slumbers on, despite the 200-ton trucks circumnavigating its face.

In fact, this giant brings me a lot of peace. We hear so much about the catastrophic things that might happen to the earth in the 21st century. Yahoo News frequently posts an item about a "global killer" asteroid that probably won't, but possibly could, obliterate vast portions of the earth. Odds are such that an asteroid would hit the ocean. The resulting tsunami would reach hundreds of miles inland, but the high ground along the Iron Range would be one of the safest places to be. I wrote a column in the wake of one such asteroid scare story and suggested that the Iron Range city of Hibbing could use our topographical strength in a slogan. "Hibbing: Probably immune to an asteroid-induced tsunami," or perhaps, "Ride the asteroid-induced tsunami to Hibbing for dry land and good times." A bit glib perhaps, but I enjoy that it's true. Then you have global warming and the threat of rising oceans. No problem. We'd have to melt the works to raise the water enough to fully submerge the bars on Virginia's Chestnut Street. Don't get me wrong. 1) We should deal with the problem of global climate change; 2) I would like to save the east and west coasts, if only because that's where my favorite TV shows come from; and 3) Who am I kidding? It *does* make me feel better knowing that whoever wins the next presidential race, I might still own dry land in 2055.

The giant's topography isn't the only story. A rare three-way watershed near Hibbing and Chisholm sends water to Lake Superior and Hudson Bay, which both feed the Atlantic Ocean, and another route reaches the Pacific Ocean through Alaska. When people first arrived on the Iron Range, thick forests of pine covered the whole region. Wildlife abounded. Lakes, in what Lamppa calls "Iron Country" were loaded with wild rice. Indigenous people learned that the ancient Iron Range was extremely cold and difficult to traverse, but they still found good reasons for people to stick around.

The First People, the Voyagers, and the Northwest Passage

Ah, for just one time I would take the Northwest Passage
To find the hand of Franklin reaching for the Beaufort Sea
Tracing one warm line through a land so wide and savage
And make a northwest passage to the sea
~ From the song "Northwest Passage"
by Stan Rogers

As in most of the Americas, people now called Native Americans represented the first human residents here. Their history on the Iron Range goes back 12,000 years to the mound builders and includes many of the great tribes of the continent. The bounty of northern Minnesota, and the special skills that peoples here had to acquire to survive, meant that nearly all societies that lived here lasted a long time and built a hearty resistance to natural hardships and outside attack. That value has entered the cultures of many different peoples through the multiple changes in land control over the last eon.

Something about the land of the Iron Range transformed the people who lived here. This happened to Native Americans and to the settlers who arrived later.

Many of the continent's native tribes can cite ancestors who spent at least some time living off the forests and lakes near the Iron Range. European influence first registered when the earliest fur trading started around 1550, but it was much later that the trade began to directly affect tribes on or near the Range. In 1640, there were about 100,000 natives living in the region scattered among almost a dozen tribes. The population of the modern Arrowhead region, including Duluth, now tops just over 320,000 people. By 1660, a powerful alliance was built among the people who would become the Dakota (also known by the more derogatory term Sioux, which comes from a French mispronunciation of an Ojibwe slur). The Dakota held the region for the next seventy years and gave Minnesota its name, from Mini-Sota for "smoky water" and the "land of the smoky water."

In 1655, the War of the Woods began, lasting until 1763. Cree and Assiniboin people from modern day Canada began encroaching on Dakota lands around Lake of the Woods (what is now the U.S. Canada border). Parents of youth hockey players on today's Iron Range might be interested to know that Warroad, the remote town with the Dairy Queen and Subway where they spend all their winter weekends, was named for the "war road" used during the most titanic intertribal war in this area's history. The Assiniboin and Cree had the advantage of metal weapons from English traders and eventually succeeded in occupying Lake of the Woods but did not press farther south at first.

Meantime, in the eastern reaches of the Dakota lands, the French began freezing the Dakota out of European goods by blocking trade with them. They preferred trade with the Ojibwe people who had begun trapping beaver along the north shore of Lake Superior. Some Ojibwe joined the Cree in fighting the Dakota. When the fighting began to affect the fur trade, a Frenchman named Du Luth held a peace council on the site of what is today the area's largest city and his namesake, Duluth. The many tribes involved did not reach complete peace, but the Ojibwe and Dakota did come to an agreement about trapping. Relations between the two large Great Lakes' tribes remained friendly for fifty years, a relationship so strong that the Ojibwe successfully made expeditions into the woods nearest today's Iron Range without Dakota objection.

We don't know how long this relative peace might have lasted without European involvement (or interference). As it was, England defeated the French in one of their many wars, closing off French access to Hudson Bay. The English, French, and Spanish brinkmanship on the continent was about empire building and the fur trade, but the factor that united these goals was the Northwest Passage. The Northwest Passage, though "real" in a sense, was at the time a purported body of water that would allow easy shipping between the Atlantic and Pacific across the North American continent. Native Americans weren't interested in shipping things from China to England, so I imagine they were quite perplexed by the giddy jumping and squealing they heard every time they mentioned a large body of inland water or a long river.

After the French lost access to Hudson Bay, they were more resolved than ever to find the Northwest Passage. This meant going through the lands of the Dakota and today's Iron Range. When they heard of a "sea" to the north and west, they increased their resolve. It turned out to be Lake Winnipeg. The French encouraged an Ojibwe attack on Dakota territory in 1736 to gain hunting grounds. The Assiniboin and Cree resumed their war on Lake of the Woods, which led to yet another long, bloody conflict on multiple fronts. By 1760, the Dakota, who had held the Iron Range region and its many resources for almost 100 years, were driven south and west. They would become best known for their conflicts with settlers and the U.S. Army in southern Minnesota and the activities of their related Lakota tribes on the Great Plains. Interestingly, crazy Horse, who defeated Custer's U.S. Army forces, had ancestral ties to the Iron Range. I was raised believing that the Ojibwe people had always lived in northern Minnesota when they are actually fairly new to much of the area. As the 19th century approached, the French population began to decline in the region as British and then American companies moved in. In virtually all circumstances, this was detrimental to the Native American tribes.

Furthermore, it turned out that Lake Superior was not the Northwest Passage. Neither were Lake Vermilion, Lake of the Woods, or Lake Winnipeg. Private and government expeditions kept moving further and further north and west looking for the passage. Something of a passage was found, but it was so far above the Arctic Circle that it was frozen solid most of the year. Many died trying to navigate this passage, including John Franklin, the Canadian explorer mentioned in Stan Rogers' song.

Changes in the 21st century revived the debate over the Northwest Passage. There really is a Northwest Passage, but passing through it is not exactly like taking a boat ride through "It's a Small World" at Disney Land. It runs far north of the Arctic Circle, and until recently, spent most of the year frozen. But global warming is opening the Northwest Passage for safer and more frequent travel by large ships. U.S. nuclear submarines have used it for decades, but the addition of reliable shipping lanes, and the ability to explore its underwater surfaces for the likely vast stores of minerals and oil, adds incalculable value to the former ice-way. The Northwest Passage lies within Canada's borders, but the United States and the Danes, among others, claim it is an international shipping lane. Russia snuck a submarine into the base of the Passage and claimed the surface beneath as Russian territory (thus, extraordinary Russian mineral wealth). Canada, not known as a military nation, is now scrambling to raise a more fearsome naval and personnel presence in the far northern reaches of its territory to solidify its claim. So we aren't yet out of the woods on geopolitical war over the Northwest Passage.

Left to the elements and their own ingenuity, humans have historically formed a natural relationship with the Iron Range. Only outside meddling dislodged people from this place. The vast resources, difficult terrain, ample waterways, and extremely diverse climate make the Iron Range an easy place to defend against the outside. These same factors isolate the people who live here. This was true for indigenous people, and it continues in our modern times.

Logging Brings Development

The *Hibbing Daily Tribune* runs a weekly history page featuring original news stories from various periods of the Range's past. The page is compiled by Jack Lynch, a veteran Range newspaperman and my former neighbor in Hibbing. Jack has forgotten more about Range history than most people my age will ever know. I'm not just using that as a cliché. He really has forgotten many interesting things. A typical conversation over the fence in our old back yard would go something like this:

Me: Hey Jack, did you hear about (name of new thing) at (name of place that closed a long time ago)?

Jack: Hmmph. (mutters). Isn't that where they buried that state senator in the concrete? Or was that Jimmy Hoffa. Hmmph.

Me: Are you kidding?

Jack: No, there was a guy that got killed there.

Me: Who?

Jack: I don't remember. You'd have to ask (name of guy who died eight years ago).

Me: Isn't he dead?

Jack: Hmmph. (mutters) I'm thinking about planting tomatoes.

I'm not making fun of Jack's; that's just how he is. Jack is retired from the *Hibbing Daily Tribune* but never actually left the building, so they put him to work compiling the history page. In the Oct. 1, 2007 edition of the *Hibbing Daily Tribune*, Jack compiled the story of a visit by R.L. Giffin to the St. Louis County Historical Society and Hibbing First Settlers Association on April 22, 1930.

According to the story, Giffin retold how he came to the
Mesabi Range in 1890:

> "As I stood upon the brow of the Embarrass Hill on the old
> tote road leading from Mesaba station west, one of the grandest
> sights I ever looked upon was in view, a veritable ocean of pine
> and a variety of other trees. I will never forget that sight or the
> impression it left upon my mind, as I stood there gazing upon
> this wonderful forest, realizing that it extended from the
> extreme eastern end of the Mesaba range to the west, about 117
> miles and practically an equal distance running north and south,
> inexhaustible, enough to last for ages as I thought at that time,
> yet within the course of a very few years not to exceed fifteen,
> this great forest was laid bare, leaving only a few scattering
> stands of pine in patches here and there."

Giffen ended his 1930 talk with this:

> "With all the timber shipped or floated out of northern
> Minnesota, very little revenue was left to build roads, or make
> improvements of any kind. However, northern Minnesota has
> benefited to some extent from the clover which was scattered
> about through the feeding of hay during the logging season."

This story was a good find by my ex-neighbor Jack Lynch,
himself a reliable volunteer for the Hibbing Historical Society.
Through the middle and late 19th century, the Iron Range had
already become known as much more than a venue for trapping
and wild rice harvesting. Indeed, there was a brief and mostly
unfruitful gold rush where hundreds of men stomped over billions
of tons and billions of dollars of pure iron ore to find trace
amounts of gold around Lake Vermilion. A few of the observant
ones noticed how their compasses danced around, and they turned

to iron exploration, though even they weren't the ones who profited from mining. At the end of the 1800s, logging provided the profits to those willing to invest in the Iron Range region. The storied forest that surrounded the Big Man Hills, the sleeping giant of the Mesabi, was mowed down. If you visit a scenic overlook today, such as the Mineview in the Sky near Virginia or the Forest History Center in Grand Rapids, you'll get an idea of what the forests would have looked like, but the truly enormous trees are all gone. Iron Range logging is much more responsible today, but no one will ever see that forest the way Mr. Giffin did in 1890.

The Iron Range Gets its Name

For some reason, many non-Rangers who move here end up in my social circles. That might be because my hobbies and interests aren't as centered on shooting or cleaning animals as is the case with other Iron Rangers, including most of my family and neighbors. Good friends and casual acquaintances alike often ask us why we stay here, how we can take the gritty culture, the resistance to change, and the lower average wages. My wife and I have always stood by our decision to stay. Our families are here. I like my job(s). Salaries are lower, but money goes farther because real estate, groceries, and supplies cost less. We often end up alone on that side of the argument, though. Many who come here think they're in for the North Woods experience, tranquil soul-building time in the woods where the only people you see are polite locals working in service industries or their out-of-town friends who visit for cross country ski vacations. It's hard for people raised on suburban trappings and vibrant city commotion to realize the appeal of the Iron Range. History comes into play once again. These new arrivals have something in common with the original mining prospectors, and for that matter, the French and English explorers who sought the Northwest Passage before them. They're missing the best part.

Who wants to talk about the difference between Iron Range hematite and other more common types of iron ore found in the mid-1800s?

Me! Me!

Right, so back then, most of the iron ore came from West Virginia and other nearby states usually known for coal. The iron ore was hard, wasn't very pure, and required lots of extra steps to convert to steel. When experts began to detect ore on the three iron ranges of northern Minnesota, they were looking for the traditionally mined hard rocks of the time. But all they found was this thick, chalky red dirt: mounds upon mounds of heavy red dirt that they threw aside, confident that they'd find the ore they sought underneath. Lamppa tells the story of one expedition that spent weeks digging away at the red dirt looking for ore. Hundreds of thousands of men walked over this red dirt looking for things they thought were valuable: gold, beavers, the Northwest Passage, trees. All of these things *were* valuable, but none as valuable or as plentiful as that red dirt.

The Iron Range was the largest source of natural red hematite ore in the world. Though dismissed at first, the ore proved to be so rich that it could be shoveled directly into furnaces to make pig iron. With the Industrial Revolution in full swing, you can imagine the implications when the titans of industry realized what had been lying around up in Minnesota all those years. At first it was simply scraped off the surface of the land. Then miners chased the ore veins underground. Then they dug huge pits, piling up massive mountains of what they called overburden along the way. Our landscape changed, but the people of the Iron Range still traversed the sleeping giant.

Historian and Vermillion Community College professor Pam Brunfelt once summarized the early years of Range mining so succinctly to me, that I base much of my following synopsis on that conversation. Over the years that followed the first shipment of iron ore from the Range in 1884, through the conversion to the complicated process of producing taconite pellets in the mid-1900s, the Iron Range throbbed with historical events and cultural electricity.

Today, being a miner is among the best jobs you could get on the Iron Range. The pay is good, the benefits are good, and the safety has remarkably improved. This was not the case during the early years. The contract mining system used then made pay inconsistent. Under that system, miners were paid only for the ore they mined. If they were assigned a bad spot to mine by the captain or if mechanical failures prevented them from doing their job, they simply weren't paid that day. The system was great for the companies because they only paid people when they were already making money off the ore. But miners could never get ahead. The system bred corruption, as many mine bosses required kickbacks from miners who wanted to be assigned productive mining areas.

Meanwhile, immigrant laborers brought with them ideas about the labor movement and believed in a better future for their families. In 1907, a major strike went out across the Iron Range. It failed. Bad feelings remained. Finns who led the strike were blacklisted from working in the mines, and they organized out in the woods. New immigrants from eastern Europe arrived and soon realized the same thing the Finns did; the system wasn't fair. In 1916, the second major strike on the Iron Range took place. Mostly, it failed too, though the contract system was weakened and World War I made the demand for ore and wages rise enough that the complaints subsided for a time. This good market continued through the war and afterward, until the Depression, which hit the Iron Range especially hard.

"Nationally the statistics show twenty-five percent unemployment during the Depression," said Pam Brunfelt. "Up here it ran seventy percent."

As with much of the country, World War II improved the fortunes of the Iron Range. Afterward, miners engaged in a successful strike, aided by a more labor-friendly federal government, that won many of the basic rights today's miners now know. It'd all be so perfect, if the natural ore wasn't running out.

Virginia Mine View

Taconite to Steel: We're Still Here

By the 1950s, even though iron ore production was setting records that would never be broken, it was also becoming apparent that the accessible portions of the ore were going to run out fairly soon. Scientists developed the process to remove the iron from taconite, which was earlier considered too low-grade an ore to be used. This process was the greatest technological innovation in Minnesota's history, way better than Post-It Notes. It provided some relief to our steel industry during World War II, but more importantly, it preserved our domestic steel industry through the latter stages of the Cold War. How does it work? Here it goes:

1. Drill the taconite shelf to insert explosives.
2. Blast the taconite into large rocks.
3. Dig and haul the rocks from the pit to the processing plant.
4. Crush the rocks in giant ball mills.

5. Grind the rocks in another mill.
6. Separate the iron from the waste, called tailings.
7. Bake the iron into pellets with other elements to make them burnable in blast furnaces.
8. Ship the taconite pellets to the steel mill.

These steps were pulled right off the wall at Ironworld Discovery Center in Chisholm, and many Rangers know them by heart.

When the process was developed, the local mining industry faced the daunting task of converting from an iron ore producing region to a taconite producing region. The 1964 "Taconite Amendment" gave taconite producers a unique taxation system where they were exempt from property taxes. This allowed them to retain the massive amounts of land they needed to mine, move, and process taconite without having to pay tax on all that land during down cycles of the steel market. Without it, no taconite mine could function for more than a few years. After the amendment passed, there was a surge of new construction on the Iron Range and an enthusiasm that hadn't been seen in a long time. Taconite plants sprung to life from one end of the Mesabi to the other. Through the late '60s and '70s, the Iron Range was strong. Cities grew, and the gutsy, traditional, community-oriented culture that could have easily died with the natural ore mines was passed on to a fourth generation of Iron Rangers.

Other changes weren't as good. The taconite process itself reduced the number of needed workers on the Iron Range through efficiency and mechanization. Even from the time of the first taconite plants to the present, efficiencies more than halved the workforce of the mining industry.

"Our primary industrial base is shrinking," said Pam Brunfelt. "I don't have a precise number, but if you look at the mining yearbooks at Ironworld, at one time in the 1920s there were 18,000 miners working here, and what they were doing was largely hand labor – shovels and pick axes and drills that were hand operated. As technology advanced, the number of workers needed declined, like in any Rust Belt area in the country, and as the industries became more mechanized, the need for workers declined."

The mines of the Iron Range faced the same modernization and globalization pains seen in the factories of Indiana, Ohio, and Pennsylvania. As machines and techniques became better and more efficient, fewer workers were needed. This tempered much of the tremendous progress made during the early taconite years and fueled another classic Iron Range cultural trait: perpetual distrust of good times. Even when the mines run, they might lay off people.

The year 1979 was the best year ever for taconite production on the Iron Range. I was born that year. My dad said that on the day I was born, he saw no reason his first son couldn't spend his whole life making a good living on the Iron Range. New trucks and snowmobiles filled the garages of miners across the Mesabi. It could be argued that the other babies and I born that year or close to it were born into an Iron Range with only two possible destinies: one of innovation and survival, or one where our pessimism and feelings of entitlement would doom us. The first test of this theory came quickly, as the steel industry floundered shortly after I was born and struggled for the first fifteen years of my life. One of these "new" plants sitting on some of the richest ore, Butler Taconite near Nashwauk, closed in 1985. Things improved in the 1990s and then worsened at the turn of the 21st century. Now they're OK, with great potential. Is this just the old up and down puppet show we've seen for a century, or is the Range really going to enter the future? A question for later.

Chisholm's "Iron Man" beside a suburban icon

Suburban Blues

Hibbing Daily Tribune, June 2006

Here's what I know about suburbs. Disaffected urbanites build nice ramblers just outside the limits of large cities to create space between them and their neighbors. These neighborhoods are so nice that everyone wants to move there. But remember, people who live there don't want to be near other people except in controlled, usually dinner party-related settings. Thus the effect of urban flight is much like throwing a bunch of positively charged magnets into a paper bag. Kaboom!

This delicious bit of irony has created some memorable modern phenomena, including road rage and the repeal of the estate tax. Driving in the suburbs means seeing exactly where you want to go and being unable to get there. You can look up and see your destination, but you must first find the correct access road to actually enter the parking lot. These roads hide below the main highway grade and seem to be named using the same process used by the John Belushi character in *Animal House* for assigning nicknames to fraternity pledges. ("I shall name you "Flounder Drive.") Though, to be fair, I don't know if folks drink quite as much in the suburbs ... at least, not in the social circles that get to name the access roads.

Here on the Range, if you see a highway, you can simply drive onto it. If there's a curb, you can drive over it. Only a handful of our overpasses are for highways; most, in fact, are for trains and mining trucks. In the suburbs, certain highways are too elite to have entrance ramps. Not here. Our biggest and best highway could be connected to a dirt road where people go to make out with their dinner dates and shoot varmints, sometimes on the same night. Maybe it's not sophisticated, but it beats feeling like I'm in a dream where I can never quite reach what I want, like I do when I'm driving in the suburbs.

I am also growing tired of the odd obsession with bears in the suburbs.

Most bears live in the woods. Suburbs often take the place of things like woods, so bears are left in a precarious situation. Do they migrate to more woods where they can resume their difficult life of hunting in order to cling to life over a long cold winter? Or do they eat tasty, inanimate things left in garbage cans right where they live now? If I was a bear, I know I'd give Dumpster-diving a good look.

Recently on *Good Morning America*, reporters gave us insight on the shocking suburban bear trend. It's a shocking trend because news agencies happened to feed several "bear in suburb" video clips to the national networks all in the same week. (Usually this footage is spaced out to provide a steady supply of manufactured suburban bear fear).

I am mostly kidding about all this. I understand that many suburbs are vibrant, culturally significant places featuring as many as four different colors of vinyl siding. Still, it's always good to get back home where our towns are separated by mine pits and wilderness rather than lines on a street map.

Aaron by a childhood Christmas tree

The Corn and the Cul-du-sac:
A Christmas Journey Home

KAXE Radio Commentary, December 2007

Sometimes you have to leave a place to realize that you really want to stay. It was like that for me and the Iron Range. I was only away for my freshman year at a college in Iowa before returning for lower tuition ... and love ... but also because I realized that I wasn't going to be able to wring out all the Iron Range from my system. That decision began to form on my drive home for the long Christmas break.

Until then, my drives through the lush eastern Iowa fields and river bluffs had been the best part about being away. These hills were pure and natural, carved by God and the gentle pressure of time. The hills of the Range were carved by men driving haul trucks and shovels, all in the lifetime of people who are still alive. I fell in love with this tarty Iowa landscape on my trip to visit colleges. I loved it still when I reported for classes. I even liked it on my first trip home for Thanksgiving. Then things changed.

A week before I was to drive home for Christmas, I was approached by a guy I'd never met. I would later learn that his primary interests were playing soccer and smoking marijuana, which I mention only because he looked like a guy who spent exactly half his time playing soccer and the other half smoking pot. Thick calves. Glassy eyes. A lot of mumbling. He came up to me and said, "So, you're from Minnesota. You can give me a ride home to the Cities for Christmas." His tone lingered strangely between questioning and declarative. My Midwestern reflexes caused me to blurt, "Well, OK then." He mumbled something and disappeared into the cafeteria crowd.

It wouldn't be that bad, I thought. I drove through the cities to get home. He seemed tolerable, a little quirky, but nothing out of the ... Dammit! I didn't get his name! I had no idea who he was. Now I was in too far. Something prevented me from asking his name after I had agreed to give him a ride, politeness maybe, or perhaps an unconscious desire for him to forget he asked me. Didn't matter. The night before the last day of finals, soccer pot guy was at my door to make sure I remembered. "We leave at seven a.m.," I said. "Aw, man," he replied. "How about, like nine."

So we left at nine-thirty for a Minneapolis suburb. By the time I had clicked my seatbelt, soccer-pot guy was cracking open a beer. He had downed three by the time we left the city limits, when he decided to switch to a better brand, chucking a half-empty can into a cornfield. Soccer-pot guy was like a lot of the people I met at this college halfway between the Twin Cities and Chicago. He talked and talked, bragged, name dropped, and cursed all the people holding him back. Not even knowing him, he seemed to be drifting through life toward nothing in particular. People like him grew up in nice houses amidst rows of identical nice houses and would probably settle hundreds of miles away in a neighborhood that looked no different. I felt bad for thinking this until he started rolling down the window to pass gas into the sharp December air every ten minutes.

We got to the Cities, navigated over I-something-94, and slipped into North Something Heightsville under the overcast afternoon sky. I dropped him off and rolled, nay, rocketed north to a place that I knew. And yes, the people of my homeland drink beer, too. Lots of it, actually. And there is farting. But we also work hard and take action. Our towns have names, real names like Taconite, Marble, and Mountain Iron. We made our own hills, thank you, and we'll make more if you let us. I'm from somewhere, dammit, and I learned this just in time for my first and only Christmas as a guest on the Iron Range.

A wooden boat belonging to the Brown family

Blight Me:
The Unique Aesthetics of the Iron Range

Hibbing Daily Tribune, April 2008

It's spring on the Iron Range. I know this because last week we had to hire a guy with a loader to remove a million tons of snow from my rural driveway. Not a plow. A loader. Hello, spring!

Maybe it's just a little bump in the road on our way to the *real* spring. When real spring finally arrives, our thoughts will turn to the stuff that's been hiding underneath that snow all winter long. The slow recession of winter's white canvas reveals old cars, rebar, scrap lumber, and sometimes even the fate of stray animals we used to see around.

Someone I know who moved to the Iron Range from a small farming town once told me about her first impression of the Iron Range. The first thing she noticed was the rather eclectic collection of cars and other metal goods in people's yards. I suppose as an Iron Range native I could have feigned outrage over this observation, but I know better. We Iron Rangers are a proud, noble people ... who leave things in our yards.

One could argue that my perspective is skewed since I grew up on a salvage yard out in Zim. As a kid, if I saw an old car up on blocks in someone's yard my response was, "What, just one?" We would walk back to grandpa and dad's shop along a path that wound through piles of aluminum cans and hulking dead machines of uncertain purpose. And this was all very normal to us, like oak trees and picket fences of Rockwell's America.

That's how it is on the Iron Range. I've heard theories that the Range's love affair with junk has to do with our working class demographics or the fact that early miners weren't able to own their own land, so they didn't mind leaving junk out. Heck, maybe we just like junk. After all, the junkyard where I grew up was just a dozen miles north of the now defunct Sanitary Harry's bar in Kelsey. The late Sanitary Harry ran for governor several times under the promise of "a car in every yard." His drinking establishment gained a reputation for the odd junk that would be piled both inside and outside the building. A friend told me the bar's owners had literally shellacked random junk to the tabletops.

The first controversy I ever encountered in Iron Range journalism had to do with a county blight ordinance. Folks in the countryside wanted the right to keep spare cars on their property so they could harvest parts when needed. But big government was getting in the way. Cabin owners were complaining and deputies were writing blight tickets. Letters were exchanged. Public outcry against the policy ran surprisingly hot. The blight ordinance is still on the books today, but I don't see any fewer cars on private properties out in the woods. I assume something of a junk car détente took place behind closed doors.

Junk defines the Range, and that's not all bad. Along the Mesabi Trail near Hibbing, tourists from all over get a good look at rusted pieces of mining equipment that were simply abandoned near their final resting places. Some might question why that stuff was left there. The answer is clear to me. All who see these scrap metal specters know that the Iron Range is a place where people shaped the land and their children long outlived their machines. And that's who we are.

I don't mean to diminish the work of so many Iron Rangers in sprucing up their yards, property, and homes. Many places around here look like the very picture of Americana. But I have to bear the truth that what many folks remember when they visit the Iron Range is the colorful, blue collar cornucopia of metal that adorns so many other yards. This sharp, rusted world is just coming into focus this time of year. Hey, I don't mind. It gives the place character.

Hibbing Mine View

Unnatural Splendor

People look, sound, talk, and smell like the land where they live. That's why Iron Rangers are hard, loud, direct people who smell like their jobs. Miners mine and smell like diesel fuel and blast powder at the end of a work day. It used to be that most Iron Rangers were miners. Now, most of them aren't. Rangers are, however, all connected to mining, either historically or directly, and it shows in the land around us. We don't cultivate land like farmers do. We dig far beyond the top soil. We blast. We tunnel. We pile. By definition that makes our relationship with the land unnatural. But after five generations, it has become comfortable. We've completely changed our landscape. In doing so, the land shaped who we are.

Outsiders often remark on northern Minnesota's natural beauty. That's a sham. In truth, no landscape more defies God's natural plan than that of the Iron Range. Whatever beauty we possess exists through some of the most brutal violence against dirt, rock, and trees ever concocted by man. Urban sprawl draws a lot of attention, but I've got to wonder if Mother Nature doesn't prefer being covered by shiny glass office buildings and theme restaurants to being shaved by lumberjacks and disemboweled by the hired hands of steel barons. Personally, I'd take a smooth layer of highways on my skin over an army of tiny Eastern European immigrants burrowing in my entrails. Fortunately, I'm not Mother Nature. I'm a guy who lives and works on earth that's been turned over by every generation of my ancestors since 1890. It's not my fault, and I couldn't fix it if I tried.

On the Range, we take a lot of pride in our unnatural beauty. We call it beauty because it's just easier that way. It's beautiful the way a crow gliding across a field after a snowstorm is beautiful. Stark. Lots of contrast. We Iron Rangers took a chunk of land bigger than most Congressional districts and flipped it like a pancake. We took billions of tons of rocks from the earth, and the only time we end up on *Dateline* or *60 Minutes* is when a mine closes and we *stop* taking that rock from the earth. And then Bruce Springsteen writes songs about the tragedy of the whole ordeal.

We Rangers usually force people to have reactions to our landscape the first time they see it. Go to the Hull Rust Mine View in old North Hibbing, and a senior is waiting there to tell you what used to be down there in that hole (iron ore) and where it went (away). "They're still working on taconite down there," one will say, "but the red ore is all gone." Then they point and say something dramatic: "It's gone!" or "All you see was carved by man!" These storytellers occasionally draw interest from the tourists who visit, but often, the outsiders leave perplexed, not only at the shear enormity of the hole, but the deep enthusiasm of the people who staff the gift shop. Think of it this way. If all a guy did with his time was dig a hole in his backyard, he'd probably be pretty insistent that visitors take a gander at the hole. "Looky that hole," he might say. "Big, ain't it? And getting bigger. You ought to see it this time next year." Though I am from the fifth generation of Iron Rangers, a generation more removed from mining than any before, I still drive almost every friend who comes to visit up to the mine to see the hole. I try to keep hip by sharing a laugh about the overenthusiastic tour guides. But should I live to be old, you just might find me there, stooped over on a stool waiting to tell a family from Indiana about what they see from the reviewing stand (a man-made crimson crater), and what used to be there (our history).

The Iron Range landscape was part of my family. The tall column of white in the northeastern sky was the ever-present cloud of steam from the EvTac plant in Forbes. I can no more remember the first time I met my mom or dad than I can remember the time I saw my first mine dump, technically called "overburden." Overburden as a word seems to be simultaneously massive and sad.

Too much burden. Got to put it somewhere else.

In more ways than one, the Range is full of overburden. Notice the hills formed by overburden and the jagged cliffs and deep pits left behind by the mining companies. Then notice the architectural overburden. Empty storefronts dot most downtown streets. Other buildings find use for purposes beyond their design, such as the Lybba movie theatre in Hibbing that is now a deli. Then, after time, see the human overburden. Spend time here, and meet a former hockey star who now sells real estate or serves on the zoning board because those are the only ways he knows to get his name in the paper anymore. See the woman who had kids early and now wonders if she'll ever see something like a real canyon or a college degree. Hear the sound of two girls singing the national anthem at a high school basketball game, one voice above the other, lofting through the gym rafters, the other earthly and common. We all know which voice's owner will return with a flourish, perhaps a bit stuck up, to the twenty-year reunion and which will spend her twenties and thirties working overnights at the nursing home, her voice in the church choir fading each year not out of age, but because of the weight of fate, jealousy, and overburden. Everyone from the Iron Range knows about overburden.

Like a lot of post-modern Iron Rangers, I left the area to go to college. This may seem fairly tame to an east or west coaster, an indistinct jaunt into another flyover state, but the subtle cultural shift was significant enough for me to realize that I had grown up someplace unique. The Mississippi River bluffs of northeastern Iowa were made by God, and it showed. They were lush, green, and were never surrounded by fences or traversed by dump trucks the size of dinosaurs. The rolling hills of Iowa were fertile, the water blue, the dirt rich enough to serve as a side dish. The well water in no way resembled tomato soup. The people were kind and vaguely aware that some time ago their ancestors came from somewhere, probably Europe. It was here that I learned how important a place can be to a person's soul. I found myself telling Iron Range stories at college parties. I recited the taconite production process to a beautiful co-ed. I'd bring up my hometown in classes and tell how the Finns were blacklisted because they organized unions. I began to sense that I was not like the other students just as I sensed the Range was not like other rural places.

At this college I took a philosophy course. For an Iron Ranger raised on a salvage yard, this was a bit of an unfrozen caveman experience. Oh, I had read about some general concepts in philosophy, but no one ever prepared me for interaction with philosophy majors, a group of people not only aware of their impending unemployment, but willing to defend it. In a class discussion, I once wondered aloud if cancer cells would hold similar ideas about their human hosts as people hold about the environment. A cancer cell can't be anything other than what it is. The time it takes for cancer to kill someone far exceeds the lifespan of an individual cancer cell. Thus, it would be hard for the cancer cell to feel bad about its existence, and, if put to a ballot, I'm betting your average cancer cell would vote "no" on chemotherapy. I fancied myself to be clever for thinking of this. Someone in the class pointed out that PBS had just aired a special on urban sprawl that showed how the growth of an urban area almost mirrored the growth of cancer in a Petri dish. I hadn't seen that show, but the cancer metaphor about summed up my opinion of suburbs at the time.

Most of my friends at this college were from the Chicago suburbs. One time I was promised a weekend trip to Chicago by a group of my pals in exchange for the use of my car. What I actually got was a trip to one of the vague northwestern 'burbs, where the houses came from a mold. All the parents I met lived there to raise their kids somewhere other than the place they were from. None of them expected their kids to live near them when they graduated, perhaps knowing that there would always be a more affluent place to flee to later. I was left knowing the Iron Range was different, but I still didn't understand the strange relationship between Iron Rangers and the land we massacre and love, my family's home for five generations.

Once a fine steak goes into the meat grinder, it becomes hamburger, and we on the Iron Range live in a hamburger wonderland. There's no bringing back our massive white pines or returning the iron to its place a mile below our feet. But sometimes hamburgers can be better than steaks, or at least more convenient and comfortable, like choosing sweatpants over a tuxedo. It may be impossible to turn mining areas back into their original state, but we do try to gussy up the rougher remainders of mining. Since 1980, the government has required mining companies to plant trees and provide for safety in former mining locations. However, the vast majority of mining activity on the Range took place before 1980. Thus, the task of rehabilitating old mine lands falls on a state agency, Iron Range Resources and its Mineland Reclamation division.

The Iron Range Resources and Rehabilitation Board was founded in 1941 to manage the tax revenue generated from iron ore production taxes on the three Minnesota iron ranges. It promotes economic development, local infrastructure, and mineland reclamation in the Taconite Tax Relief Area. This includes present and former mining locations spanning from Grand Rapids to Ely and south to Crosby and Ironton. In short, this agency is supposed to fix all that was put asunder, both physically and economically, over 100 years of gangbusters mining on the Iron Range.

I sat with Dan Jordan, director of Mineland Reclamation, to find out how they fix areas that have been mined. He works out of two offices, one of which is housed at Ironworld in Chisholm where I met him one morning. Ironworld is what it sounds like, an interpretive park, museum, and entertainment venue celebrating the extraction of iron ore from the ground. It was built on top of a reclaimed underground mining location from the old days and overlooks the cliffs of a mine pit dug somewhat recently. At one time, it featured a wide array of attractions, such as "Pellet Pete's Mini Golf," remote control Lake Superior ore ships, and actors playing old time characters from Range history. Many of these are now buried somewhere in a pile of financial overburden, but the place still serves as an entertainment venue and a solid testament to Range history, even though the building is slowly, and quite literally, sinking into the collapsing underground mine shafts beneath.

When I called Jordan to set up the interview, he directed me to go to the second building at Ironworld.

"Mineland Reclamation used to have a sign, but it was really old, and they made us take it down," he said. "They called it blight."

Kind of ironic, I said.

He paused. "Yeah."

Jordan had prepared a useful packet of information about his office and the history of mineland reclamation in the area. Before its inception, mines had almost no rules governing what they did with abandoned mining areas. They would leave behind gaping mine shafts full of water that went half a mile into the earth. Rusted pieces of equipment would be left in the precise spot where the motors stopped working. Then legislation created provisions for safety, and Jordan's job began. He told me how they used to block up the old mine shafts by building a road out to the locations big enough for concrete trucks to pass. Then they'd cap the shafts with concrete and drive out.

"The problem was that we were building roads to quiet, abandoned locations, which for local kids is like an invitation that says 'party here,'" said Jordan. "I could just imagine some kid out with his babe on a Friday night who decides it'd be good to show how cool it would be to go jump on this concrete. It wasn't a good situation."

The solution Jordan and his team found was a manufacturer who made a white synthetic foam product. Ten men carrying sixty-pound bags of this foam could hike to an abandoned mine shaft, unload their packs, and watch as a chemical reaction caused the foam to expand and harden in the shaft opening. Cover it up and suddenly you've reclaimed a mine location without creating the kind of secret road system coveted by teen gangs, mobsters, and people who *really* don't want to pay to get rid of those tires.

Jordan told me a story about the foam. Miners at Hibbing Taconite reported seeing kids playing on the edge of a cliff overlooking a mine pit near the mining location of Kitzville. Similar calls kept coming in over the next few days, so he and the state mine inspector went out to see what was going on. The area in question wasn't accessible by road, so they borrowed a barge from the mining company and floated their way out to a location near where the boys were spotted. They then hiked a difficult path over to a spot where they could clearly see signs of human activity. Eventually, they came across two boys hanging out in a mine shaft tunnel that was dripping water and mud from its crumbling ceiling.

The boys said they had walked as far as they could on the other side of the pit by Kitzville and swam the rest of the way to what they considered a pretty cool hangout. Since having children die in a shaft collapse is an explicit no-no in mineland reclamation, Jordan and the inspector told the boys not to play there anymore, and they came back later with the foam to fill in the tunnel. But the foam, as I stated, is bright white and highly synthetic. The resulting white blob was now clearly visible from all angles of the pit.

"We brought a rock from the site into L&M (a local hardware store) and had them color match the rock so we could paint the white blob," said Jordan. "We went out one day and painted it." They brought some white and black paint, too, to speckle the fake rock and create an even more convincing façade. Now you can't tell the difference when you look out at the pit from afar.

There you go. Maybe you can spot the fake rock next time you visit Kitzville.

A poster on Jordan's wall reads, "If it can't be grown, it has to be mined." A mild-mannered model state employee during most of our chat, Jordan showed the most passion when he asked me a hypothetical question. "How many mined minerals do you find in a Pepsi can?" I've never been asked that. My mind was stuck on iron, and I knew pop cans were made of aluminum, so I froze up. I couldn't get past what I knew about the pop machines at local mines, where the companies demanded that local bottlers provide steel cans. Jordan waited for my answer, but all I offered was awkward silence. "Five," he said. He named them. Aluminum was one. I heard him say phosphorus. I missed the next two because I forgot how to spell phosphorus. "Titanium is the one everyone misses," he said. "You can't have white paint without titanium." Everyone? I got the sense he asked a lot of people this question. Jordan knows how many elements are in a lot of things. After he explained this to me, I finally got to the question I was hoping to ask. How can a conscientious Ranger come to peace with what we've done to the land where we live?

Jordan paused, though not quite as long as my Pepsi can pause. "We have to be wise stewards of our resources," he said. "With the population the way it is, we can't go back. If you want to return the Iron Range back to what it was, it's not as easy as filling in the holes. Give us your washing machines, your cars – that's where our earth goes."

In the first eighty years of mining on the Minnesota ranges, people were extracting pure iron ore. In other words, almost every ton of what left the Iron Range on trains was turned into the steel that fed two world wars and the industrial growth of the world's only superpower. Even now, our ore indirectly feeds the growth of China, potentially a rival superpower in this modern era. About four tons of extra material is extracted when one ton of ore leaves the region, the aforementioned "overburden" of the taconite generation. So he's telling the truth. You can't go back. Stopping where we are now means surrendering the livelihood of the whole area and, in a larger sense, stopping the flow of elements that create our manufactured goods. "Environmentalists don't understand that if it weren't for the thirty-nine minerals in their computer, they couldn't send me an e-mail telling me not to do my job," said Jordan.

We are what we are. We dig. But we are no less a vibrant example of the human condition. We could live lighter on the land, returning our refrigerators to their rightful home on the edges of Keewatin, Chisholm, or Eveleth. Things would get ugly, though. Where would we go in the morning if our job at the coffee shop was lost because the art buyer lost her job when the nonprofit shut down because the Wal-Mart closed when the Ford plant folded after it was determined that steel was too rough on northeastern Minnesota? Would we play cards? How many elements are in a deck of cards? Probably more than you think.

The Iron Range does not grow like the suburban cancer we discussed in that philosophy class. In fact, the Range is fixed in its borders: west to Grand Rapids, east to Hoyt Lakes. North stands the wilderness of the Chippewa and Superior National forests and Boundary Waters; South lies the tamarack bogs of Zim, Meadowlands, Floodwood, and Aitkin. Cancer moves outward in a circle. Its strength is in the newest part of its expansion; its core is undesirable at best and empty at worst. That's not how it is on the Range. We are a jagged red line that runs west-southwest to east-northeast. Along the line, the property values are cheap, the schools are great, and the economy is sketchy. You can't get a good bagel sandwich, but no one cares about that. The Iron Range could lose all of its people but could still be seen from space. It spans across a finite natural ore reserve, so its geographic expansion halted almost 100 years ago. 100 years from now, it will still rest in jagged lines on hard earth that, because of market conditions, we can no longer afford to mine, crush, and ship. The only question is whether the people will find other things to do once we've finished digging our holes.

The Iron Range is not like a cancer. It is like a cut. Some cuts are lethal, but if they aren't lethal, they follow a predictable pattern. Over the course of 100 years, a geological half-blink, people cut the earth. They cut it so deep that the men in the pits felt the heat of the earth's core. But when the cutting stopped, as it did on the Vermilion and Cuyuna ranges, and slowed as it has on the Mesabi, the wound would not spread like Starbucks and strip malls of the outer suburbs. We Iron Rangers know where the Range's permanent boundaries lie. We look around and see ourselves as hard-working people who ride booms and busts. We mop up the bloody mess, the taconite, and try to hold it all in.

You see, they took it. They took the iron from our earth, which was the only reason most of our families came here. We stand over this cut and try to hold in everything except our sole commodity, the earth beneath our feet. We sell this commodity for peace and comfort and the betterment of our children's lives. We try to hold in our jobs, our children, our traditions. If we are a cut, maybe that explains our aversion to change, and our fear of "bacterial" outsiders. It troubles me that one of three things happen to cuts that fail to kill. Sometimes they reopen, painfully, and you start over. Other times they heal, either leaving a scar that the host will explain at parties ("This is from when a bunch of immigrants built a nation") or, in some scenarios, the cut heals so completely that no one ever knew it had been there.

That last scenario is what scares me most.

I like the dumps. The pits are pretty. Behold our unnatural splendor. You may laugh at my exuberance if you wish, but it is ours. God didn't make our landscape, nor could He fix it in as many years as we dug it up. But I know He could fix it soon enough, turning the life we live here into a story told by my great-great granddaughter in some futuristic city.

I don't want to be just a story. I don't want this cut to heal. I don't want the Iron Range to pass away.

So, we dig.

Stairs from a North Hibbing house site

Bad Publicity? Not so Fast

Hibbing Daily Tribune, October 2002

I haven't heard this much talk about the latest issue of *National Geographic* since I was in sixth grade, and everyone on page forty-eight was totally naked.

The October 2002 edition of *National Geographic* profiles Hibbing as part of the magazine's monthly "ZIP USA" feature. The piece, written by Sean Elder with photos by Catherine Karnow, highlights Hibbing as the home of Bob Dylan, a town struggling against a rough economy that has sent many of our young people away.

You can definitely tell the chamber of commerce didn't write the story, but we all saw that coming. You can't expect a national magazine that routinely photographs the most amazing things on earth to call our resident strip mine "picturesque." The story is slightly slanted toward the negative, but it is all together honest.

A few people I've talked to were pretty riled up about the little yellow magazine after they read the story. I don't see the cause.

Hibbing is what it is. We live here by choice, and most of us truly like life on the Iron Range.

The fact is that a national publication devoted a hefty amount of ink to our small town. The story showed the world that, A) we're Bob Dylan's hometown, B) The Greyhound Bus Museum is open for business, and C) we're located near the great outdoors. We would have paid hundreds of thousands to get this message out in an advertisement.

You might not like that the story pointed out that many young people leave our area, but don't pretend for a moment that this isn't fundamentally accurate. Young people leave small towns to strike out on their own. Many find opportunity elsewhere, but many others come back and build a life in the community they grew up in. Such is the fate of any small town. If we had more jobs to offer, we'd get more young people back. The publication of a magazine feature story makes this statement no less true.

I mean, come on. It's not like they said we were a town populated with Caribbean pirates. And once you've either nodded or seethed over the story, you can remark on the many cool things in the *National Geographic* feature.

In the "On Assignment" section of the magazine, Catherine Karnow spoke of her experience shooting pictures in the lunch trailer at Hibbing Taconite. A picture shows her playing hearts with some burly miners dubbed the "alpha males." It's a cute image, but the break of a lifetime for the person who took the photo, Cliffs Mining Services public affairs coordinator Steve Zeitler.

Zeitler said he carries cheerful memories of how the big city photographer charmed her way through the lunch crowd at HibTac. His photo shows some of that story.

In the "Field Notes" section on the Web page, Elder points out his favorite thing during his time in Hibbing as the viewing of a Hibbing Community College play. We all knew director Mike Ricci and the theater gang did a good job, but it's nice to see them get a rave review from a publication you can actually buy on Broadway.

Ricci told me that Elder and Karnow spent hours photographing the theater's production at the time, *Sly Fox*. As Elder took in the show, Karnow shot every conceivable angle in the theater, from the audience's viewpoint to that of the actors as they stepped on and off stage.

Afterward, Ricci spent more than two hours talking with Elder, who quizzed him about his background, the theater community, and all things Hibbing. Ricci said he asked if any of the interview or photos would make the cut. Elder told him "probably not." Apparently, he knew the editors were looking for a Dylan-themed story, so even the author knew he was laboring in vain. But the HCC theater group got a plug anyway, as Elder wrote that his night at the Hibbing theater was one of his best while in town. "I was pleasantly surprised to see that in the field notes," said Ricci.

In another part of the magazine, we see a photo of the Golden Crest Healthcare Center's cane hockey team, The Golden Eagles. This photo ran in the "Final Edit" feature, where photo editors include pictures that didn't make the cut for their respective story, but are interesting anyway. It's nice to see cane hockey finally get the respect it deserves.

Best of all, they spelled our name right: Hibbing. As the old saying goes, there's no such thing as bad publicity, as long as they spell your name right.

Joan Baez and Bob Dylan (photo from National Archives)

Bob Dylan in Hibbing:
The Saga Continues

Hibbing Daily Tribune, October 2004

Hibbing's most famous son just released an autobiography. It was big news – on the cover of *Newsweek,* touted in *Rolling Stone*. These are national magazines. Near as I can tell, only a couple dozen copies of his book were sold in our town. This column is the first time Bob Dylan's *Chronicles, Vol. 1* has been mentioned in this, our hometown newspaper. The book came out twelve days ago.

Such is the quirky mystique of Bob Dylan in Hibbing.

I talked to Mary Keyes, who co-owns Howard Street Booksellers in downtown Hibbing. They sold all seven copies of their supply of Dylan books on the first day and several more the following week when they received more from the publisher. "That's a rush for us," she said. Still, Keyes said the Dylan "rush" only beat the rush for Bill Clinton's recent memoir by a few copies, and Bubba's not a Bluejacket. Keyes said they weren't sure how locals would react to the Dylan book, since so few overtly display affection for our Iron Range folk troubadour.

Meanwhile, our local Wal-Mart didn't carry copies of the book. Perhaps someone at the regional distribution center failed to realize that Store #2937 is near the boyhood home of Bob Dylan. Many of the Dylan fans I spoke to ordered copies online.

As much as we Hibbingites try to get attention for our high-quality, industrially-zoned real estate at affordable prices, we've actually had far better success in getting our name in front of about a hundred million people as the home of Dylan.

Over the past couple years, I've watched as articles about Dylan and Hibbing appeared in some of the largest, most-read, most-respected publications in the world, ranging from *National Geographic* to the *New York Times*. Sure, some get cranky because the articles aren't puff pieces. To the writers, our town appeared to be a rough Iron Range city with population decline and a streaky economy. Of course, we know the truth is that we also have two Hardees. Oh, wait. Not anymore.

I have to keep things in perspective. What if Bob Dylan decided to buy a house out on 25th Street and move back to his hometown? What if he spent the rest of his days sitting out front in one of those collapsible lawn chairs, playing his guitar and answering questions for anyone who bothered to ask? What if he wore an "I (heart) Hibbing" t-shirt at all times? Somehow, that wouldn't seem quite right either.

So, if you're so inclined, check out Bobby Zimmerman's new book. Even if a majority of Hibbing residents never get excited over the fact that one of the most influential musicians in the last fifty years got his start right here, there's got to be a few who, like me, find some sense of hope in that.

Korean and Vietnam Wars plaque outside of Hibbing High School,
"ERECTED TO HONOR THE YOUTH OF THIS SCHOOL"

Times of War

Regardless of your politics, region, or religion, the 9/11 terrorist attacks became a touchstone for the generation of Americans who were in high school, college, or just starting their careers at the time. And though I don't know exactly where that twisted steel we all saw on the television screen came from, we can assume that at least some of the original ore came from the Iron Range. We know that our ore fueled world wars, provided heft to new technology, and, in short, played a physical role in the development of our nation.

Our nation remains at war.

> *"In times of war, things thrive up here. It's really good for the economy to have the mines going full bore. I think that's part of the reason people [on the Iron Range] are so gung ho about war."*
> ~ Bill Schleppegrell, Sr., retired German teacher at Hibbing High School, World War II POW

When you watch the television news at night, you see major wars, major cities, and major people, all important and usually distant. But the truth that has spanned human history is that these major events, and the people they affect, spring from small, seemingly less important places. Places like Hibbing, a town of about 18,000 which rests in the center of the Iron Range. People like the Schleppegrell family, who have lived in Hibbing since 1952.

Every town should have a couple like Bill and Norma Schleppegrell. Civically engaged, with countless volunteer hours for one cause or another, the Schleppegrells seem to be everywhere. They are well into their retirement; Bill from a teaching career, Norma as an administrator and advocate for mental health issues. I see the pair at community plays, political events, and open forums all the time in Hibbing. If I don't see them, I wonder where and how they are. They always say hello, they always ask about my family, and they do the same for the hundreds of other people they know and see each day. When they were named the grand marshals of the "Mines and Pines Jubilee Parade" in 2003, the community rejoiced. Spectators of the largest parade in the Range's largest city cheered for them as honored citizens who define the generosity of human nature and remain the greatest walking advertisement for the Catholic Church I've ever seen. But I never knew the whole story of their family until I stopped in for a visit at their apartment in 2007. Norma poured me a hot cup of coffee with a touch of Bailey's. Bill was recovering from a fall, but he was still thinking ahead to curling season.

"What strikes me," said Norma, "is that this is the place where, in the 1970s, people were egging our house."

"And making obscene calls at all hours of the night," added Bill.

Norma continued, "I even had people tell me they didn't think Bill should be able to teach at the school anymore. And we're the ones twenty years later riding down the street waving to everyone in the parade as Grand Marshals."

"I was sitting in the back of that car," said Bill, "wondering who in the crowd egged our house."

"Even to this day," said Norma of the Vietnam years, "I wonder. Those weren't kids calling the house then; they were adults who called, threatening our son. It was a very tumultuous time."

In 1943, Bill Schleppegrell, a young Army Air Corps pilot from northern Minnesota, was shot down over Germany during a bombing mission. He was taken prisoner and spent the rest of the war in a German POW camp. After the war, he got a degree in education, met and married Norma, and spent his whole career teaching German, the language of his captors, to Hibbing High School students. Twenty-five years after Schleppegrell's release from the POW camp where he practiced his German amid torture and squalor, his son Bill Schleppegrell Jr., who had joined the Army against his family's wishes, laid down his gun in Vietnam, refusing to fire another shot. He had endured weeks of sacrificial night missions into enemy territory designed solely to increase, both actually and sometimes artificially, the number of enemy dead reported to command. Through miracles of love and the unexpected cushion of bureaucracy, he was allowed to return home, but with wounds no one could see. Today, more than thirty-five years later, both father and son of the Schleppegrell family oppose war in principle, the Iraq war in particular. Both have spent most of their lives living on the Iron Range, a place where the revenue from the steel that fueled every 20th century American war paved our streets, built our schools, and unified the immigrant groups who mined the requisite iron ore.

The Iron Range knows war well, providing both steel and soldiers in large quantities. During World War II, the enlistment rate on the Iron Range, spurred by the large immigrant families hungry to prove their loyalty to their new country, was, by anecdotes and limited data, as high as or higher than anywhere else in America. During Vietnam, when students across the country were protesting the war, chapters of "Kids for Uncle Sam" sprouted up at Iron Range high schools. These last six decades of American wars shaped and scarred the Schleppegrell family. Their opposition to the Vietnam War, including the anti-war organization of their late son Larry, and the conscientious objection of their son Bill Jr., put them at odds with an Iron Range society that usually saw war as both necessary and patriotic. Today, Bill Jr. still becomes anxious when he sees vehicles with lights on at night, the way U.S. patrols drove down dark Vietnamese roads, still sees people hiding in the woods when he drives down a country highway in northern Minnesota, far from the old battles.

Bill Jr. told me this at Checco's Tavern, a place that is both dark and full at three in the afternoon. After we shared a pitcher of Hamm's beer, a Checco's specialty, and some pleasantries, he told me that he had finally been approved for government benefits for his posttraumatic stress disorder.

"They finally figured out that I'm more than fifty percent crazy," he said. "They're finally saying what I knew all along."

Bill Jr. grew up the oldest of seven in what he described as a strict Catholic family.

"We said the full rosary every night. On Friday, we got to say the rosary in the car on the way to Dairy Queen." In Catholic school, Bill Jr. got a butch haircut so that the nun couldn't pull his hair. After years of gaining attention as the class clown, he said he decided to do what was considered the best thing a boy in a strict religious upbringing could do, which was go to seminary to become a priest.

"Being a priest was above being President," said Bill Jr. "But after a year and a half at seminary, I was kicked out. I was a little too loose on the rules."

Back at Hibbing High School, Bill Jr. worked nights and weekends at Crippa music store and learned to play guitar. Dabbling in the popular folk music of the early 1960s, he later transitioned to rock 'n' roll and spent his last years of high school playing with a band in bar gigs around the Iron Range.

In late 1968, Schleppegrell Jr. got a call from Selective Service saying that he would likely be drafted within the next year. By enlisting early he could stay home through the holidays. "So I enlisted," he said. "And later at basic I learned that they were trying to show support for the war by boosting enlistment."

From teenage years of rebellion, Bill Jr. found quick acceptance for his choice to join the Army.

"It was a very good, very patriotic thing [to join the Army], second to being a priest," said Bill Jr. "It was the Army of the Lord, or the other one. My parents were scared. Dad was a POW and knew what it was about. I just said, 'what the hell,' I get a paycheck and out of Dodge. I was excited to join. I was proud to be in the Army. I was doing my duty. I was a soldier."

He came home on leave in January 1969 to find that there were even more benefits.

"I was nineteen. Every place I went in uniform, I didn't have to buy a drink. Everyone loved you because you were a solider. Being a soldier was just as good as being a priest, but you got served beer younger."

Then he was sent to Vietnam.

"When you get there, it's a whole new ballgame; it's a war, dead people are involved." Trained as a mortar gunman, Schleppegrell's unit didn't have any armored gun vehicles. Instead, he was assigned to be a gunner on an armored personnel carrier. "No one rode in that bus," he said of the vehicles he rode on. "If you hit a bomb, you're toast, so everyone rode on top. So they'd have a chance."

Like many Vietnam servicemen, Bill Jr. became acquainted and frustrated with the politics of the war's tactics and the way arbitrary decisions meant life or death.

"We were supposed to be killing people, but we hadn't seen anyone, so they weren't happy. Someone thought that if we drove at night, we'd scare up something."

It was these night patrols that shaped the younger Scheleppegrell's harsh memories of the Vietnam War.

"They were picking us off," he said. The turning point for him came one night when North Vietnamese soldiers were popping up between American tanks and firing at both. "We had our third platoon wipe out the second platoon," he said. "You don't drive down the middle of the road with lights on to kill people. They kill you. But they needed to show that we were in battle. And we needed to be in battle."

So the next morning, Schleppegrell Jr. decided to object. "I refuse to bear arms," he told his commanding officer, a specific military offense. He was reprimanded and days later told that if he signed an Article 15, accepting responsibility for disobeying orders, that he would be busted a rank but wouldn't be court marshaled. He refused. Court marshal proceedings began. Schleppegrell Jr. was put on house arrest at the main base camp, spending his days working in the kitchen or guarding things of little value. He didn't know if he would go home freely, in handcuffs, or in a box.

Back in Hibbing, letters between Bill Jr. and his mother Norma underscored the drama going on at home.

"A young priest from Duluth was sending a letter around to all the high school graduates telling them they had an alternative to going to the war, that they could be conscientious objectors," said Norma. "He offered draft counseling. We thought it would be a good idea to invite him up to our youth group, so we did, and it was a horrible evening. The parents showed up and just took this man apart. We didn't think that would happen. We thought people would listen and make up their minds, but that didn't happen at all. It was just awful. Well, meantime, our second oldest son Larry got very involved in all the anti-war movement in this country. He let his hair grow, refused to cut it. He was the first boy in Hibbing with long hair. People egged our house. People marched down to the bishop to complain. The school board agreed to pay for him to get classes at the university to graduate high school because they were afraid the other kids would grow their hair long.

"So Larry and his friends and some others put on a peace rally in Hibbing – the first – and about 100 people showed up, and it never made a paper. [State Senator and later Governor] Rudy Perpich came and spoke at the rally, and it never made the paper. You can go back in the archives, and you'd never know that it happened."

For the next few years, the Schleppegrells found themselves on the fault line that tore apart almost every small patriotic town in America during the Vietnam War. And while they lost friends, faced scorn from some, and endured late night calls threatening their son, the letters from Bill Jr. in Vietnam became even more troubling.

"He'd grown up on the Iron Range that was so patriotic and just joined the military," she told me. "When he got over there, he realized that what they were doing was morally wrong. And so he refused to shoot a gun. He writes us a letter saying he's going to be court marshaled. I got a hold of John Blatnik [former U.S. Congressman from nearby Chisholm], and he had me talk to a woman in his office who told me they had a desk full of these kinds of stories. This was at the time when Nixon was saying that we weren't in Cambodia, and Bill said our guns were pointed into Cambodia. Bill said when they knocked over a rubber tree they paid the owner $300 but if they accidentally knocked over a Vietnamese civilian they paid the family $30. These things really affected Bill. It's left its mark on him his whole life."

Bill Jr. was not court marshaled. He spent five months under house arrest in Vietnam. His mother's pressure on Congressman

Blatnik led to a psychological exam that declared him to have a "situational anxiety disorder." He was put on Valium and relaxants, which he said was "anything but fight motivating." Eventually, he was given an honorable discharge for medical reasons. "And it was all because I didn't sign that Article 15," he said. "If I had signed that, I'd have been screwed."

He was flown out of Vietnam on a TWA flight and arrived home before his letter that held the news. He didn't sleep for four days because of all the cars driving down the street. They had their lights on. "It was as scary being home as it was over there."

Bill Jr. has lived a lot since he came home from Vietnam, but he still panics when he sees vehicle lights at night. His life has been marked by the difficulty of readjusting. Back at Checco's in downtown Hibbing, Bill Jr. laments Minnesota's recent 2007 ban on indoor smoking. "There's no hangout for the dissidents anymore." He points to his jacket, which has a Vietnam veterans pin on it. "I wanted to forget I was in the Army. I was ashamed I was in the Army, but if I heard someone talking about being in the Army, most of the time I could tell he didn't do what he said. It didn't happen that way. Now I wear the pin so that the John Wayne types know not to make it up. The real John Waynes don't talk about it."

He paused, finished his glass of Hamm's. "You know, the Range was the same then as it is now, largely defensive about war. There's something wrong when they say if you're not killing people, you're not doing your job. [In modern war] you're not fighting across a street. There's no front line – same as with Iraq now. We like to think we're all hard working and patriotic, but it's really terrible. I think our military should protect us, but I don't want to see my worst enemy sent over there. Not for reasons like [Vietnam and Iraq]."

Bill Schleppegrell, Sr., patriarch of his large family, took his time in the German POW camp, an experience that literally wiped his memory clean of the weeks and months prior to his crash in Germany, and built a philosophy that relies heavily on forgiveness.

"It's all part of my outlook on life," he said. "I came to realize in my study of Germany that people are mostly the same as anywhere else; it's the leaders that can bamboozle them."

Thousands of Iron Range students learned German from a man who would have every reason to hate Germany, Germans, and the language used to interrogate him as a young man. As I was preparing to leave their apartment so they could get on with their busy day, he quoted the German writer, Thomas Mann, who of the First World War wrote, "War is only a cowardly escape from the problems of peace." And you could see how in an Iron Range bar somewhere, a blowhard could, well, blow hard against the implication of cowardice in a patriotic war. In truth, only a family like the Schleppegrells could know what war actually does and how hard it is to repair the aftermath. On paper, they lost no one in a war, but they did not escape the effects of war. Bill Jr. still battles his memories from that war. And today, they watch as war keeps coming through the television, now with a ticker along the bottom of the screen tolling the casualties at all hours.

"I think war has certainly left its mark on the Range," said Norma. "I don't know if it's for good or bad. In World War II, we all thought we were doing the right thing. Then Korea was forgotten, then Vietnam became about hippies, and so much division took place. People want to be loyal. People want to put signs out saying they support the troops. But it's hard for some to understand that you can support the troops but be against a war."

"The most surprising thing to me is that so many people didn't learn a thing from Vietnam," said Bill Sr.

Teachers want to see people learn, but I can only imagine how the stakes change when the lesson is war, and war marks the darkest times of your family's history.

I am not a veteran, only a few in my family ever served in the military. To the best of my knowledge, my family has not claimed a combat veteran since Bull Run during the Civil War, when by family legend, my great-great-great-great-grandfather lost an eye to a lead ball fired by a rebel solider. But living on the Iron Range means living in a world full of military veterans. They are hawks and doves, Republicans and Democrats. Some supported the wars in Vietnam or Iraq, others opposed. In short, they represent society at large except in one key way: they know what war really means. Some believe war to be a necessary evil; others believe war to be just evil.

At the community college where I teach, many recent Iraq war veterans now join my classroom. Some share their most vivid combat memories with the class and others mention their service only once with no detail. I tried to get some of the veterans I met to share their perspective for a radio program on Veteran's Day, but even those most willing to share stories in class were unwilling to go on the radio. At first I was disappointed, but then I thought, "What do veterans trying to rebuild lives back home have to gain from this?" The war in Iraq is not a war here, it is a political issue. Because so few back home know about what has been described as the fog of war, it's very easy, often preferable, to avoid the topic entirely.

"People who know, know," said Bill Schleppegrell, Jr. of combat. "People who don't, don't. I'm against the war but I'm not against the guys fighting the war."

Not everyone who knows war agrees about what it means or whether it should be waged. I could have probably found an equally honorable Iron Range family that supports the war in Iraq.

That same family might have supported the war in Vietnam. But I am left pondering the grim statistic that most of the iron our parents, grandparents, or great-grandparents mined during the early 1940s or the late 1960s is buried somewhere in Europe or Southeast Asia. I am strangely comforted that our iron products today largely serve other purposes, like building cars, skyscrapers, and bridges, even in the countries we once fought.

We live in a large, powerful nation that requires a military to protect itself. So long as this is true, we rely on the service of people willing to risk their lives for any mission deemed important by leaders in Washington. We deal with the leaders on Election Day. During other times, we should take note of the silent scars of war on our human landscape. Not all casualties can be seen plainly. America remembers and duly honors those who lay down their lives for their country, but in places like the Iron Range, we see those who did not die or get shot, but carry the burdens of war the rest of their lives. They also sacrificed for love of country.

For a region often deemed "isolated" by sociologists and "remote" by travel writers, the Iron Range, its land, and its people, play a vital and complicated role in wars, politics, and the American story. We provided most of the steel and some of the soldiers that freed Europe and Southeast Asia during World War II. America went back to Southeast Asia for Korea and Vietnam, again with Iron Range steel and soldiers, only to battle to a stalemate that lasted until just recently. I think it was about 1989, when I was living on our junkyard, that I watched *Alvin and the Chipmunks* sing about the fall of the Berlin Wall on our fuzzy color television. I was probably nine, not privileged but comfortable enough, and proud to be an American. I owned buckets of green plastic army men, some of which were perpetually frozen in a falling motion after being shot or hit with flak. I never thought of these green men as dead, but I usually set them aside. I had no idea what to do with these men who were neither dead nor alive, casualties yet to be determined. I hear stories from some of the students I've met after they came home from Iraq, or from Bill Schleppegrell Jr., or from his mother Norma, who worked with veterans at a local mental health center, and they put words in the mouths of those green army men frozen in fall on the battlefield.

"I talked to one man, an officer, who was so proud that he got all his men home," said Norma. "And they're home, but five have DWIs, two committed suicide, and so on. All these struggling veterans are living with us now, and there's a feeling here that implies they should just get over it. Maybe that's everywhere."

Today Iron Range steel goes to China, India, and around the world. Wars are different now, but we Iron Rangers are still here. Some are veterans of World War II and others raised a family working overtime during the 1940s. Some fought in Vietnam, some protested, many more went to school during those years. Today, Iraq veterans return home quietly every day. Though our generation might be defined by the Iraq war, actual veterans comprise but a small minority of our population. Most of us have no idea what war really is. The evening news remains grim and significant, but this place and our people still linger below the headlines, living on the thin line between war and peace. Things change slowly here, but I hope that the Iron Range of my children's time prefers peacetime to war. That is how it should be. War may perhaps be necessary at times, but times of war are never good.

Lost and Found

KAXE Commentary, May 2007

This week, I lost a whole box of geraniums off the roof of my car when I forgot to load them after buckling Henry into his car seat. I didn't realize it until I was miles down the road. I could have gone back, but I knew those geraniums were gone for good. Life has taught me that every loss brings a potential find. What you find isn't always what you lost, but it's usually of equal or greater value.

Once when I was a kid, grandpa pinned a silver sheriff's badge to my shirt the moment I arrived for a visit. It was one of those great kid moments. At the end of a long autumn day of playing in the leaves, it was time to go home, but the sheriff's badge was nowhere to be found. I never did find the badge, but I still remember how meticulously my whole family combed the leaf-filled yard looking for it. Though I didn't realize it then, that memory was worth more than the badge.

When we lose things, it's not the absent things that upset us; it's what the things mean. For a twenty-four hour period after our son Henry was born, I lost the memory card with all the digital pictures. I had backed them up on our computer, but there's something about losing the original record of your first son's birth that makes people treat you a little bit more like Hitler than they otherwise would. I found the card under our computer desk, but the scare was real.

My wife Christina told me about an essay she wrote for school when she was twelve entitled "The Island of Lost Things." Gnomes would take your things to this island and try to use them. If the item had no use they would toss it back to the regular world where you might find it later, thus explaining why you sometimes found lost items but not always. That makes as much sense as any other theory.

Perhaps, as some couples find with brief separations, it can be good to spend some time apart from your lost things. Our son Henry experiences this all the time. He'll play with his favorite toy for days before eventually hiding it somewhere for safe keeping and forgetting it. Then, as with his toy road grader this morning, he finds it later and acts like he's received a brand new toy. "I can't believe it," I imagine his toddler mind saying. "I used to have one just like this!"

That's the real reason professional movers can pack a house in less than a day when it takes the owners a week to do it themselves. As you empty drawers and move furniture, you find things that you thought to be lost, and you have to take a moment to appreciate them. Hey, remember when these shirts were cool? Whoa, we still have the Atari. I wonder if it works. Oh wow, it does! And suddenly it is 1987 all over again, and "Centipede" is the best video game ever produced. And yes, these things are just things, but losing and finding them is still somehow more satisfying than the impossible task of keeping them at our side forever.

Lost and found is much more than things. You can lose hope and find it again. We thought our terrier Molly Dog was gone when she fled into the rural wilderness near our home, but we found her and realized how important she was to us, despite her barking and inappropriate grooming habits. We lose loved ones, but find memories and ways to move on. And every loss – each dog, flash drive, watch, relative, friend, lover, and shoe – is necessary for us to find who we are. Losing is lousy, but finding is what it's all about.

There will be more geraniums, and I will take better care of them in the future.

An Iron Range sunset

True Knowledge
in the North Woods

Hibbing Daily Tribune, May 2008

The other day, my almost-three-year-old son Henry and I walked down to our lake to throw sticks, a favorite pastime of Henry's and a ritual that has begun to grow on me. We normally throw rocks, but our multiple April blizzards covered all the rocks with cold water. So we've been throwing sticks lately, different because they drift back to shore to be thrown again. You don't get the satisfying "splunk" sound, but the whole endeavor is much more sustainable, without the sharp rocks underfoot this summer. It's kind of like driving a compact car instead of a Mustang. You get high off the ethos, not the pathos.

Henry is highly focused. I hope this means that in the future, he will focus on kindness to others and getting a job after college, but for right now, he focuses squarely on throwing sticks into the lake while northern Minnesota's natural world unfolds around us. On this one particular day, that world included loons.

You don't realize how little you know about loons until you explain them to a toddler.

"Ducks!" said Henry.

"No, not ducks. Loons. They're a little like ducks but, uh, different."

"Ducks!" he repeated.

"No, loons. They're Minnesota's state bird. They're black and white."

"I throw sticks," Henry concluded.

Four loons appeared in front of us. Two of them danced on the water, flapping their wings the way birds do in nature photographs in magazines. Was it a mating ritual? I assumed those birds were the males, but was it three males wooing one female or were these two pairs of loons fighting for habitation rights to the small lake by our house?

"Look, Henry. Those loons are dancing."

"Ha," said Henry. "Those ducks funny."

I know people who know what those loons were really doing. I wouldn't know where to begin. Sure, I could stuff my brain full of loon facts only to be left with another question. What was that other bird that was swooping down at the loons on the lake, presumably protecting its nest near the shore? That bird has a name and story, too, as do all the other birds Henry and I saw that day. And you know, even after a lifetime in northern Minnesota, including a failed career in the Boy Scouts, a college botany class in which I received a B-, and literally hundreds of observations by wily old timers, I still hesitate before identifying tree species.

Basswood? Plausible.

I know a lot of things. I know the historical dynamic of every presidential race of the 20th century (the taller guy always wins, except when named John Kerry). I know the name of the talking horse from *Hot to Trot*, a movie starring Bobcat Goldwaith that I watched on VHS at my grandma's house when it was a new release (Don. Just Don). I also know more than I should about adult contemporary hits of the 1980s and '90s thanks to my stint as an overnight disc jockey during high school. I know all these things, and yet I did not know what those loons were doing on the lake last week. Not for sure, anyway. I would have traded hundreds of things that I know for that one thing I did not know at that moment.

We don't know as much as we think we do. The more I learn, the more I realize that I don't know much beyond the tip of my nose, if that. No one can teach this lesson better than someone young, short, and curious. The very next thing I do after writing this sentence is to Google loons. I need to know more about loons and most other things.

Light pole and sidewalks in North Hibbing

The Iron Range Today:
A Guide For Travelers, Packsackers,
and Prospectors

"We do everything a little differently. And if you look at it geographically, we speak a different kind of language than the Twin Cities, we're in a different weather pattern than the Twin Cities or even Duluth, we are [fifty or sixty] miles or more in any direction from any big city, and we're our own little world. We operate that way most of the time."
~ Craig Hattam, history teacher at
Hibbing High School

The Iron Range is a collection of small towns, all connected by cultural and economic traditions along a jagged streak of iron ore under the "big man hills" of northern Minnesota. Big city newspaper reporters and passing tourists often use words like "gritty," "hardscrabble," or "rough" to describe these towns, but locals would be quick to point out that these critics must not understand all the work that went into the decorative downtown flower baskets. Just north and south of these rough, gritty, hardscrabble towns lays countryside as beautiful as any in Minnesota. Out there, people live in large lake homes, charming split entries, or trailers covered in old tires. Township governments rule these rural areas, though some locations are listed on county maps as "unorganized." These citizens answer only to county officials too cash-strapped to monitor them. Attempts to enforce zoning or open bottle laws in vast portions of the Iron Range region are thus met with exasperated local displeasure. "I always drink the first one in the truck and the rest at home, and these two-by-fours are for whatever I damn well want to build!"

Our Range towns and townships do battle from time to time, especially during the high school hockey tournament or when politicians divide the annual pot of mining tax revenue. But throughout history, they have united for important things. Usually, they vote the same way in elections (an economically liberal, socially conservative, quasi Libertarian brand of Democrat). They've learned to stand together for working men and women during collective bargaining and strikes, especially after early 20th century mining strikes bitterly divided communities. And these towns all hold a remarkably cohesive culture based on outdoors activities, unobtrusive faith, hard work, school pride, and a deep distrust of rich people and outsiders. At the same time, the strange strung-out geography of the Range creates pockets of isolation, so much so that someone in Town A takes offense at being compared to the rabble over in Town B, even when everyone involved is wearing a Polaris snowmobile jacket and steel toed boots. Indeed, though one can characterize the overall Iron Range culture, each town offers its own unique flavor.

Everyone's hometown is known for something. Big cities have widely assumed reputations. Chicago: wind and prohibition-era gangland violence. New York: a city-state with a vibrant culture and a bad attitude. Los Angeles: freeways and plastic surgery. Rome: romantic, but also very dirty. Toronto: somewhat large and presumably Canadian. Small town characterizations aren't as sweeping. I had a friend in college from Freeport, Illinois, whose high school's sports teams were called the Pretzels because the town's German immigrants cooked many pretzels. The high school went without a mascot for years until they decided to name the teams after the pretzels cooked by an old lady during games. My friend was a swimmer who vividly recalled the placement of the Pretzel logo on the back of her swimsuit.

Ever heard of Buhl Water? It's a well-known bottled water, chemically similar to Aquafina, Evian, or Holiday Pantry, and it comes from Buhl, a little town smack dab in the middle of the Mesabi Range. I've consumed this water. It passed my standard test for H_2O: no solids, clear, and cooler than any part or parts of the human body. I got in trouble once for making fun of Buhl, but Buhl and I get along great, now. Right, Buhl?

Meantime, Hibbing is "the town that moved" in the 1920s and again in the 1940s and '50s to accommodate mining companies. Spend an hour with anyone over the age of seventy, and you will hear where their old house was in North Hibbing and where they rolled it on huge timbers to the South, or "New", Hibbing. In the process, men accidentally dropped entire hotels and tore a brand new Carnegie Library to the ground because it couldn't be moved. During its glorious years of growth in the 1920s, and again in the '40s and '70s, Hibbing became the unofficial capital of the Iron Range, the town where mine bosses lived and the finest shops were located. Though Hibbing remains the Range's most populous town, its retail economy has since settled below that of Grand Rapids on the far western Iron Range and the quad cities of the eastern Mesabi as consumer traffic pushed outward toward Highways 2 and 53. Thus, from time to time, you will encounter a city-wide attitude in Hibbing somewhat similar to that of an aging Miss America, still pretty but not "1978 pretty."

Hibbing stands in contrast to nearby Chisholm, a blue collar town that developed mostly as a home for miners and *not* their bosses. Even today, as science brings us to the doorstep of flying cars and robots that can change diapers, people in Hibbing and Chisholm still think that people in the other town are up to something. They're not sure what, but something.

The "Quad Cities" serve as the eastern population base. Virginia is the "Queen City," named after popular transvestite RuPaul. Ha! No, not that kind of "queen," though that's the joke on which high school sports rivals lean heavily. Virginia was actually a logging center long before it was a mine town. Today, it's often the first Range town that visitors see because of its location at the intersection of state Highways 53 and 169. The first impression that most brand new visitors have of Virginia, and thus the Range, is: "Holy crap, they have a lot of bars here." Two solid city blocks of bars line downtown Virginia. Other towns have plenty of bars, too, but not as many and not as close together.

Eveleth, situated on a massive hill south of Virginia, is the hockey capital of the U.S.A. and home to the largest hockey stick in the world, a claim disputed by owners of a giant Canadian stick. Until the end of the 20th century, Eveleth had two water towers, one painted with the words "Eveleth Hot" and the other with "Eveleth Cold." Many children on the Iron Range grew up believing that water temperatures were actually controlled in the towers. When both of Eveleth's towers began to fail, city leaders replaced them with a sleek, modern water tower that lacked such whimsy.

Another of the "Quad Cities" is Mountain Iron, the location of the first iron mining on the Mesabi Range. Water towers grabbed headlines in this town before, too. When they repainted their water tower, they used the abbreviation: "Mtn. Iron" instead of the previous and commonly used "Mt. Iron." City leaders said they were tired of hearing tourists pronounce it "Mount Iron" instead of the proper "Mountain Iron." I am waiting for the day when a visitor to the Range tells me, "Yeah, I drove here past that town, what was it, Mitten Iron, er, Montana Iron. Something like that."

During the boom years of the iron mining industry, Gilbert, the fourth of the Quad Cities, was known as the "wet" town, where drinks flowed freely and you might be able to find a woman. That reputation continued even after the boom towns of the Range became permanent and decent women moved in. It didn't help that Gilbert is home to one of only two functional strip clubs on the Iron Range. As a sixteen-year-old pizza boy, I delivered a box of chicken fingers to a dancer *while* she finished her act, an experience that will probably flash before my eyes when I die. As Gilbert's centennial approached a few years ago, some townsfolk wanted to stage something called "Whorehouse Days" to attract national attention to their small, economically troubled town. City leaders balked, mostly at the notion of willingly associating their name with whores, and managed to block the Whorehouse Days group's permits. To date, you can still see defiant "I am a Whorehouse Days supporter" bumper stickers on Iron Range vehicles.

Speaking of defiance, Kinney literally seceded from the union in 1977, in protest of increased federal aid for foreign nations while the town couldn't receive any help with its failing water system (Kinney, ironically, is a few miles east of Buhl). The town formed a "military," elected a "president," and started selling "passports" (All in quotations, because the military primarily marched near the town's bar, the president was really just the kindly, but feisty gray-haired mayor, Mary Anderson, and the passports were fundraisers for what became the annual town festival, "Secession Days"). Unfortunately, enthusiasm has waned over the years, and the town has given up on its dream of independence. Many described the 2007 death of Anderson as the ending of an era on the Iron Range.

The western Mesabi, where I live now, is a little different than the rest of the Range. For one thing, the western Range towns are in Itasca County. Something about the county line changed how these cities developed. Some of the richest ore in the formation lies near Nashwauk and Keewatin. These two towns share a school. My mother's family comes from Keewatin, a small town that has always served as a bedroom community for miners. Though we grew up in the country, my sisters and I remember fondly our time spent in Keewatin visiting our grandparents. I marched through Keewatin dressed as a penguin and, once, as Donald Duck, for the annual Fourth of July parade.

Nashwauk, slightly larger (they have a Dairy Queen), lies to the west. My family lived in Nashwauk for a short time when I was very young. In fact, my earliest memory is of my dad and I watching city crews pave the alley behind our house, marking what was then the edge of town. Today, that alley still represents the edge of town, but locals are talking about a taconite mine and steel plant facility that may be built nearby.

Farther west, towns like Pengilly, Calumet, Marble, Bovey, Coleraine, and Grand Rapids comprise the rest of the Western Mesabi. All of these towns owe their existence to early iron mines, but none of them have had any mining activity in more than forty years. Grand Rapids in particular often rejects the term "Iron Range" because so much of the town's economy depends on wood products like paper. A nebulous line exists somewhere in Itasca County between the classic "Iron Range" and a hybrid wood-products and tourism-based Iron Range. Hey, we're all good people, but sometimes these waters require delicate navigation.

To me, the Western Mesabi is characterized best by Bovey and Coleraine. Now that a new highway bypassed Bovey in 2007, travelers don't get quite the same experience. Here's how I remember the trip. Drivers would approach by Highway 169, slow down at the hill that leads into Bovey, look up at the massive pile of overburden that separates the town from an old mine pit, make a ninety degree left turn by Bob's Country Market and Liquor, and drive past a sign that has the classic picture "Grace" of an older man praying over a simple meal of bread. Then drivers made another ninety degree turn, and WHAM, you were in Coleraine staring down a four-lane freeway that leads to Grand Rapids. The Bovey experience forced every motorist to think about life just a little bit deeper. I don't blame the state for the bypass. It was really unsafe to combine a liquor store parking lot with hard ninety degree turns.

Like any region, all Range towns vary in their appearance and zoning laws. Newcomers are usually stricken by physical characteristics first. Rangers take a strange pride in displaying their excess vehicle fleet around their homes. At the same time, elements of Range cities sport unique architecture and ornate buildings from the Range's fast growth during the early decades of the 20th century. The strange combination of crystal chandeliers in the Hibbing High School auditorium, and the abandoned washing machines on vacant lots furrows the brows of most any newcomer, while passing unnoticed by most true Rangers. But once you've come to expect this paradox, you can begin to understand the people and culture that have allowed it to rise.

Hibbing High School

The Many Faces of Iron Rangers

The three physical elements of a story are setting, plot, and characters. Our setting speaks for itself, with tall piles of overburden, blood red dirt, scarred land, and the deep contrast between evergreen forests and dark blue lakes. But a fuller story of the Iron Range explores why the people who live here wear "Old Fart" mesh-back ball caps all year round. Well, not all of them. Sometimes it's a NASCAR hat, the coolest jacket from the 1992 J.C. Penney catalogue, a red plaid hunting shirt, or a lime green blouse purchased at a defunct downtown store that now houses a tattoo parlor. Iron Rangers are not image people. When *North Country* was being filmed on the Iron Range, a casting call went out for extras. The filmmakers gave simple instructions: show up at the Thunderbird Mall in Virginia dressed like it's the late 1980s. More than one witness said that they could barely detect the clothing differences between the people who showed up that day and the people who show up any other day.

I've learned that on the Iron Range people distrust a shirt and tie much more than a greasy pair of overalls. For instance, I often wear khaki pants instead of jeans. It's not a fashion thing or part of a dress code; those are just my pants of choice. We moved from Hibbing into the country a couple of years ago, and after my third or fourth trip to the county canister site where we bring our garbage, one of the ladies who punches the tickets said, "You must have a really important job, you're so dressed up." This was at the dump. Everything I was wearing, except the khaki pants, would have been rejected by the Salvation Army store. But for most Iron Range men, khakis are for funerals, retirement parties, and dates with women too fancy to marry.

More important than physical appearance, fashion, or fads, people of the Iron Range tend to value practicality in their lifestyles. They also tend to value economic equality over the "keeping up with the Jones'" mentality. Politicians are judged on how they handle themselves in the bar, rather than in the media. People pick a contractor through word of mouth much more than through reading the classifieds. Everywhere you go, everyone you talk to, the conversation begins with an exchange of stories about people both of you know. If you don't know the same people as everyone else, you need to fix that. When Bill and Norma Schleppegrell came to Hibbing in 1952, Norma was befriended by Bob Dylan's mother, Beattie Zimmerman. "Bea called and said, this is what you need to know about Hibbing," Norma recalled. "She said don't talk about anybody when you come to the coffee party because everyone there has a relative in town. And in fact they did. There were twenty-four women there, and I was the only one who didn't have a relative. Bea told me that if anyone asked, I should tell them I was her cousin, because you needed a relative."

I teach communication classes for a living, including interpersonal communication, where we talk about the process of perception and stereotypes. I don't want to necessarily run down the many stereotypes outsiders have about the people of the Iron Range. By now you've probably figured out a few for yourself. So, I'll give the obligatory statement. Not all Iron Rangers wear jackets promoting their favorite brand of snowmobile, work at a mine, spend every Saturday night in a bar, smoke or chew, communicate with their children only on fishing trips, race stock cars, use tanning booths in unsafe amounts, or keep nine guns in a case for hunting and one gun above the TV for when the government comes. But I know a lot of folks who have one of these traits and a few who possess all of them, enough so that I'm not worried about these people thinking I was talking about them specifically. At the same time, you just can't count on people matching their appearances on the Iron Range. Because Rangers value a level socioeconomic appearance, if not actual outright equality, that stereotype you see walking down the street could be the town's mayor, doctor, drunk, or dog catcher. Maybe all four.

Like many Iron Rangers under the age of forty, I have hipster friends who live in the Twin Cities. Between sips of $5 lattes, they will sometimes call me just to ask, "What *is* there to do up there?" Sometimes, this is followed by chortling and references to something they read in the A&E section of an alt weekly.

Well, I'll tell you the same thing I tell them. The Iron Range is full of excitement if you're willing to cast off your black turtleneck and get elbow deep in nature, human drama, and working class pleasures. For those not yet familiar with the area, I make no promises about your trip to the Iron Range, other than you will experience something interesting if you keep your eyes and ears open. Unless you plan to bake a pie, leave your BlackBerries at home. Join me in a place where coffee is weak but usually free. A place where the most popular wall arts depict our towns' main streets back when people shopped there. A place where Bob Dylan, Kevin McHale, and Rudy Perpich are all equally famous in their hometown of Hibbing. A place where there are more organizations dedicated to saving old closed theatres than there are open theatres. A place where millions of dollars were once spent on auditoriums, parks, and the humanities and now are spent on economic development consultants. It's a blue collar world, rich with sincerity and irony, where worldly cynics predict our imminent demise and small town optimists foresee a return to the glory of the red ore days. These forces live in an eternal yin-yang. Neither will prevail, for they draw upon each other for survival. Uncertainty clouds the future, so you best just have some potica and tour one of the most unusual places in the country.

Hibbing's Greyhound Bus Museum

Our Past is a Big Deal

If you go by what the media says about us, all we have here on the Iron Range is taconite, hockey, beer, and sexual harassment. Well, we also have museums. I've talked plenty about Range history, but I've found that the best way to enjoy the Iron Range of today is to become intimately aware of its past. From west to east, the Iron Range celebrates its unique past with displays and dioramas. You can see wax men recreate the early labor movement, back when we kept the country alive with steel. You can find out about how a little taxi service began its long transformation into the nation's largest bus company.

In Calumet, see Hill Annex, the only state park dedicated to an abandoned mine. The attached museum display is a solid look at how the mining process worked back in the day, but the real treat is to take a guided tour of the mine pit showing the way these massive manmade lakes were dug and filled with water. The tour guides can tell you about how pumps regulate the water in the pit, something true of many pits across the Iron Range. In fact, if humans just disappeared one day, many of the developed parts of the Iron Range would flood within a year or two. So far, we've been able to keep the pumps running. Hill Annex may not sound like a state park experience, but any kid in Minnesota who wants to get his or her book stamped at every state park must also go to Hill Annex. Not only are there no bears, but the bears were all killed with swords by eastern European immigrants sometime around 1912.*

(* I'm making up the part about swords, but the no bear part is real.)

In Hibbing, the Greyhound Bus Museum, America's only bus museum, details how a little Hupmobile that chugged between a mining location and Hibbing eventually became the nation's elite Greyhound Bus Company. This museum has the unfortunate distinction of appearing every other year or so in a nationally syndicated newspaper column or anti-tax organization press release as a woeful example of government pork. The museum was built and is still operated through the hard work of Hibbing's Gene Nicolelli. Nicolelli raised much of the early money to build the museum, first housed in the Hibbing Memorial Building, and later moved to a new facility in historic north Hibbing, a street that has since been renamed "Greyhound Boulevard." My favorite part about the museum is the chance to just sit for a moment on one of the old buses. Imagine what it must have felt like to be on that bus going from Toledo to St. Louis to get a job in 1936, or to ride from Detroit to Minneapolis to see your best girl in 1956. How many characters in how many stories rode these buses? Of course, visitors can bask in the irony that Greyhound hasn't come to Hibbing in a decade, and our only other non-local bus service stopped coming in 2007. The bus museum truly captures a moment in history that will not be seen again.

Not all of the museums are quite so specific. Many towns have small historical society museums or at least some sort of public display. Ironworld and the Iron Range Research Library is a one stop location for Range history. Ironworld is one of those strange places that you have to see to believe. The giant facility sprawls across hundreds of acres overlooking an enormous mine pit. Seen from a boat on the pit, it would look like the kind of place a James Bond villain would hide his stolen nuclear warhead and train his jumpsuited minions. It was built and for many years operated by the State of Minnesota through funding by the Iron Range Resources and Rehabilitation Board. Former Gov. Rudy Perpich originally envisioned Ironworld as a grand interpretive center honoring Range history. However, in the years that followed his administration, the facility overreached, with enormous cost overruns and poor attendance. In high school, many of my friends worked in the ethnic food pods at Ironworld, with few customers and bizarre stories of eating raw chicken sandwiches to conquer boredom. Now Ironworld has reorganized under a nonprofit group with financial help from Iron Range Resources. Despite the sometimes valid criticism of the early days of Ironworld by naysayers, the place has become a splendid facility, with a classy outdoor amphitheater, fascinating exhibits on the region's history, culture, and the clearest public explanation of the taconite production process I have yet to see. This isn't like some of the historical museums you might find in flat land places where the highlights are the year they figured out how to grow wheat and the year they got a stop light. Range history is decidedly more complex, like the backdrop of a good novel. Writers, poets, and thinkers would find much to consider between the lines of our historical markers.

Food and How to Get it

There was a time where a good number of Iron Rangers depended on wild game as a staple of their diet. Those days have long passed, but many Iron Rangers still depend on deer hunting season as a way of getting the hell out of the house (or getting someone else the hell out of the house).

Contrary to the stereotype, we don't eat just venison and iron ore here, though there is so much iron in the water that newcomers often go months without a bowel movement. We have a proud tradition of ethnic foods, good restaurants, and a unique night life. It's true that we tend to eschew night clubs and dance halls for bars and … additional bars. And while some social elitists might scoff at the many ma and pa greasy spoon diners dotted along the Range, we have several restaurants that I'd take over any big chain or fancy fare. In my native Hibbing we have Zimmy's, which is probably the world's only Bob Dylan themed bar and restaurant. This place serves as the hub of "Dylan Days," Hibbing's annual Bob Dylan celebration. Identifying their entrees is much easier than identifying songs at a Dylan concert, though many of their menu items are named for Dylan songs or lyrics. In Gilbert, the Whistling Bird provides a high class Jamaican dining experience to an Iron Range clientele. To go there is to see a paradox. The owner (a real Jamaican!) has become so accustomed to reassuring the meat and potatoes people who live here that "the spice is on the side" that he now greets diners at the door with that exact message. The place has excellent atmosphere and routinely pops up on "top restaurant" lists in statewide publications. When they filmed *North Country* on the Iron Range, Oscar-winning actress Charlize Theron hung out at the Whistling Bird. For me this cements its place as a strange portal between the Iron Range and high society, where Hollywood and hematite collide.

Another interesting twist on our mining towns is that most have at least one Chinese restaurant. Steve Potts, a history instructor at Hibbing Community College, tells his classes about how you can spot an old mining town without ever seeing its mine pits or abandoned underground shafts. Chinese and Vietnamese restaurants often followed mining operations during the late 1800s and early 1900s because it was one of the few vocations available to Chinese immigrants after the transcontinental railroad was completed. In Hibbing, we have two Chinese restaurants and one Vietnamese place. Virginia has the same. They change owners every once in a while, but usually between Chinese families who have been in the restaurant business for generations. I conducted interviews for this book at the Hong Kong Kitchen in Hibbing which I've always considered a classic Iron Range tribute to Chinese fare. They recently announced a move to a new location to add an all-you-can-eat buffet, the inevitable outcome of any ethnic restaurant attempting to do business with Scandinavian-Americans. Now, many authentic Mexican restaurants are cropping up as America's current largest immigrant group slowly makes its way into our region. And don't forget our many classic ethnic Range dishes, like Cornish pasties, sarmas, lutefisk, Indian fry bread, and the pizza from Sammy's, which is just pizza, but from Sammy's.

Beer is also a big deal on the Iron Range. Beer is like liquid bread, something that can serve as a suitable base for any combination of things you ingest orally.

Most of what I know about beer is gleaned off the side of cans. And as soon as those words leave my mouth, I realize that I can't really recall much of it other than, A) It takes me twenty minutes on the exercise bike to work off a Busch Light, and B) I don't care.

As an Iron Ranger, I hear the word "beer" more often than I hear the word "oxygen." Growing up, there were two coolers on the front porch at family gatherings. One had pop for the kids, the other had "barley pop" for the adults. This rather ambiguous amber liquid played a role in many family conflicts, but now, in adulthood, I've come to enjoy the comfortable taste of beer(s).

Regardless, it's a mistake to think the Range only offers burger and beer joints. Though, if you like burgers and beer, we've got you covered.

Adventures in the Great Outdoors

In case I've left the impression that shooting, eating, and drinking is all we do on the Iron Range, I'll offer this. Our woods and lakes provide much inspiration for photographers, artists, and writers. To the bafflement of many of my red-blooded relatives and friends, these attributes of the Iron Range are more my speed. Almost every rock, stick, and leaf in Northeastern Minnesota has been documented by one or more of these artists. The result can be seen in a decorative wall calendar or charming local coffee table book, both available for $24.99 at a store that sells candles, stuffed bears, and signs that read "Welcome to Our Cabin." But the really interesting aspect of the Range is that most of our towns feature stores like this *and* bars that still use urinal cakes depicting a Vietnam-era Jane Fonda. Viva la difference!

Yes, the Iron Range offers fast access to the outdoors. Home of the Mesabi Trail, you can cycle, run, rollerblade, or ski along the spine of the Mesabi Range, between the skeletons of old mining equipment that was literally too big to throw out. The Mesabi Trail, under construction for more than a decade, will soon span the entire 132-miles of both the Mesabi and Vermilion iron ranges. Most of it follows old railroad right-of-ways, so bicycling along the trail will give you the same view that a traveling chunk of iron ore would have passed on the train. The Mesabi Trail is designed for riders of all skills, though I must admit some portions of the trail ascend massive 100-year-old piles of mining overburden.

For several summers, until our house exploded with babies, I rode in the Great River Energy Mesabi Trail Tour in August, an informal bicycle ride featuring numerous corporate sponsors. My favorite feature was the rest stop sponsored by the Minnesota Iron Mining Association, where riders are offered snacks and FREE taconite pellets to carry with them on the rest of the ride. Nothing enhances athletic performance like a pocket full of rocks.

The annual tour is a fundraiser for Independent Public Radio stations in Minnesota, such as 91.7 KAXE in Grand Rapids, where I am a contributing producer and essayist. It attracts people from all over, especially the Twin Cities. It's a family event, not a race, but that doesn't stop people from breaking out the Spandex.

Spandex is the kind of thing that just violates so many cultural norms on the Iron Range. No one looks good in Spandex. Naturally, that applies to lumpy folks, but it also goes for good looking people with rippling muscles and pleasing curves. Good looking people end up resembling the guys from some futuristic movie where people are created in tubes and social class is distinguished only by the color of your jumpsuit. Meantime, "regular" people end up looking like a week's worth of dirty diapers in a tall kitchen trash bag. Here on the Iron Range, if men or women want to show off their bodies outside, we prefer they wear cutoff jeans and tank tops like our ancestors.

Our great outdoors has always had the most appeal for the moderately to significantly sedentary among us. We've got lakes for fishing, woods for hunting, and even if you don't want to kill critters, both lakes and woods offer many options for sitting and resting enthusiasts. In the summer, I-35 North coming out of the Twin Cities and U.S. Highway 53 North coming out of Duluth are choked with boats, campers, Illinois license plates, and car dealer decals from Forest Lake, Burnsville, or Eden Prairie. These people and their well-dressed trophy spouses come to fish on the big lakes that are listed in the fishing books and to pump the locals for secret lakes where they can get an edge on the other temporary visitors. You should know that all bait shop clerks and owners in northern Minnesota keep a list of lakes they're willing to tell you about and a list they would not divulge even under threat of torture. Unlike residents of popular travel destinations like Las Vegas and Florida, Iron Rangers actually embrace the same pastime as our tourists. Fishing and hunting remain central to both the local economy and our local culture.

A&E on the I.R.

Arts and Entertainment. Our arts and cultural activities on the Iron Range aren't quite as vibrant as those of big college towns or classy urban downtowns, but they exist with a great sense of earnestness. Also, because we're a working class area where entertainment dollars are limited, you're more likely to see arts experiences that are accessible. The quick growth and shady political dealings of most of our early towns left places like Hibbing with enormous and expensive auditoriums that other working class locations could never dream of acquiring. As a result, the quality of arts on the Range usually exceeds expectations if you're willing to watch the papers and find things to see and do.

You can always count on festivals, parades, and street dances dedicated to the honor of mining, some kind of produce, or a tragic but quirky event that gave a Range city pride in itself. A good event nails all three. These summer traditions are really about personal memories. For instance, I'll always associate drunken, smoky Iron Range street dances with the night I hit it off with my wife and mother of my children. The night we first took an interest in each other was so magical that we didn't notice the din of cover bands and leather-clad street fighters at the Hibbing Mines and

Pines street dance. We returned in subsequent years to recapture the magic, only to be disappointed that the setting was better suited for finding the high school classmate who never quite got over graduation than it was for finding one's life mate. Thus, in our memories, our meeting became all the more fateful. We all have our own favorite memories of Iron Range summers. I can't promise visitors that they'll find a spouse at "Pick and Shovel Strawberry Great Fire of 1913 Days," but they might find a good beer.

I've realized that a true understanding of the Iron Range can only come from experiencing the heat of summer, the cold of winter, and the friction of people co-existing along an iron formation in a place known only to national weathercasters as the "Upper Mississippi Valley." There are people here, friends. And the stories flow like water.

The biggest mistake visitors to the Iron Range can make is to turn up their noses at the human elements of the area and focus only on the nature. The glory of this place is the odd way nature, its resources, and 100 years of immigrant laborers crashed together to create a place unlike any other and utterly irreproducible. Don't come expecting quaintness or for the locals to dance at your beckoning. If you do, someone may punch you in the face, and you'll deserve it. It's much more entertaining to come here and watch someone who didn't read this get punched in the face. Also, you can get a good meal, an education, an affordable domestic tap beer, and a lesson in humanity. Come join me on the savagely beautiful red rock peaks of the Iron Range to see what travel magazines fear to report.

Our Vices and Virtues

Outside Minnesota, only a handful of things identify us to the world at large. Mining and Bob Dylan usually rank near the top. To a lesser extent, our labor movement past remains important in some circles. But in recent memory, the only really big national splash about the Iron Range came from the 2005 Oscar-nominated movie *North Country*. The movie depicts a story based on the real ordeal that many women faced working in Iron Range taconite mines during the 1970s and '80s. Many might bristle at the scenes in the movie, but a woman who worked in the mines during those years told me that every one of them happened to at least one woman in real life during the bad years.

Long before the movie came out, a book called *Class Action* by Clara Bingham and Laura Leedy Gansler was published and caused a minor stir in Iron Range circles. I read the book around the same time I saw the first production of Eve Ensler's *The Vagina Monologues* in Hibbing. A group of community women presented the play at the Hibbing Community College Theatre. At the time, the series of short monologues had gained national attention on Broadway and was being presented in college theaters across the nation to raise awareness of violence against women.

For those who don't know, the play explores the social stigma associated with saying the word "vagina" aloud, which, to many, is an offshoot of gender equity problems throughout society.

To me, the notable thing about the performance of the monologues wasn't that local people accepted the public utterance of a "taboo" word. It was that women appeared to have finally carved out something close to equal status in Iron Range culture. Twenty years prior, maybe even ten, this performance would not have been allowed. Even if it had, it would have been met with howls of protest. The play's producers and directors would have been labeled with horrible, non-polite names for defending the performance as a call for gender equality. While there had been some murmurs of discontent by some in town about the monologues, most respected the right of the production to continue.

I can't say that we have achieved complete gender equality on the Range. A significant majority of our elected officials and business leaders are still men, and a "good old boys" attitude still dominates some circles. But we're getting there.

Class Action explores the rough transition some women experienced when they were first hired to work alongside men in the mines. The case was controversial, and many miners felt they were wrongfully labeled as chauvinists. But the fact that harassment took place in several instances cannot be denied.

Because of the working class, generally male-dominated history of the Iron Range, gender equality in our region was trailing the rest of the country. This wasn't anyone's fault; it's just a fact. And like racial integration in the 1960s and religious tolerance after the 9/11 terrorist attacks, we continue to make progress after terrible setbacks.

"When women professionals come into an area like this, it's more about being included in the culture," said Lisa Vesel, a public relations professional on the Iron Range who moved here from out of the area. "You're excluded when everyone goes out hunting, and I think that's anywhere like this, not just here. However, this is such a strong tradition in our area, and women can easily be excluded by not being part of the club."

The club. The system of people's personal connections and common activities. Our unique style of social networking for political and social strength on the Iron Range is, at once, the thing that unites us and the thing that often prevents meaningful progress; not just for women, but for young professionals, new residents, and people of varied ideologies and religions.

The question is, how can we achieve such progress while retaining the many virtues of the Iron Range? We are a place of natural and unnatural beauty, where some of the world's most picturesque sunsets are enhanced by affordable beer and sometimes gunshots. Our people are real, most of them value honesty more than wealth. Iron Range schools provide the heartbeat and life's purpose for Iron Range towns. We shouldn't leave these traditions behind, but we also must accept change. Even slow change would prevent the social stagnation that could one day wear our communities down to the nub. I just hope that change goes well with the popcorn they sell at youth hockey games at the Eveleth Hippodrome.

Henry enjoying an Iron Range snowstorm

Frozen Locks Confound Modern Life

Hibbing Daily Tribune, January 2005

The human race has accomplished impressive feats in its relatively brief time on Earth. Among the favorites: fire on demand, the cotton gin, abstract thought, and horseless carriages.

But for every amazing triumph forged by people, nature lays waiting to offset our gains.

Our story begins with a New Year's weekend ice storm. I was quite grateful for the heat that comes from what we moderns call "radiators" and the water that comes from "pipes." A similar storm would have surely killed my ancestors, who lived in caves and clubbed animals for food (circa 1936).

Anyway, the storm created a thick layer of ice over most cars. By the end of the weekend, the water that melted refroze in the general vicinity of my car door locks.

When a natural phenomenon renders a modern convenience totally useless, you get a new perspective. An advanced internal combustion engine perched atop a steel frame crafted to withstand enormous strain is really just a "neo-boulder" when the door locks are frozen, a neo-boulder that collects calendar parking tickets.

For the benefit of others, here is a step-by-step guide to thawing your car door locks if they freeze. Remember, this is based on my experience, and probably not the only way to solve the problem.

Step #1: Turn the key hard ... no, no ... HARDER!

Step #2: Lament your "pathetic, wussy writer hands."

Step #3: Attach hair dryer to extension cord. Blow air on lock. Sub-zero temperatures will keep air "warm," but never hot. Results similar in effect to slowing the advance of a glacier with the warmth of your own naked body. It might work but no time soon.

Step #4: Use de-icing spray on lock, door, and hinge. Again with the key. Again with the turning.

Step #5: Kick door. Curse. Louder. The neighbors have small children? Tough.

Step #6: It's just a lock. Have some cocoa. Calm down. Look for solutions on another modern invention, something our president calls "The Internets."

Step #7: Using solution from Internet, heat key with lighter until very hot. Insert key in lock. Turn.

Step #8: "Aaaarrrrrggggghhhh! Jack Frost, I will find your home and somehow light it afire using the fur of your house pets as kindling. Lo, ye shall rue the day your icy finger touched this lock." Kick door again. Curse again.

Step #9: Turn on the Weather Channel. Review long-term forecast. Next warm day projected for July 8th. Weep softly.

Step #10: Day 2 – you're rested and ready. Acquire heavy duty heat source from friend. Technically, it's designed to "strip paint," so be sure to let the pulsing fog of desperation completely absorb your mind before proceeding.

Step #11: Lose argument with spouse over use of heat gun. Modify nozzle on deicing spray to get farther into the frozen lock mechanism.

Step #12: Six long, cold days after the ice storm, the door is unlocked! Oh, joyous times!

Step #13: The unlocked door is frozen shut. Repeat from Step #1 – this time with gusto.

It's not much, but I hope it helps if you're ever in the same situation. Meantime, remember to never let modern devices diminish your respect for nature and its ability to make us look like morons for days on end.

Oh, Deer! Not Again!

Hibbing Daily Tribune, October 2003

One night, my wife and I were discussing hunting. I said: "I'm not against hunting, but I don't want to kill additional animals when I can get plenty of cheeseburgers and chicken fingers." It was a quaint personal belief statement on which I could base my decision not to hunt even though so many of my friends and family do.

Early the next morning I was riding high on my moral stance as I drove to work in Superior. It was dark. There were a lot of bushes on the side of Dupont Road.

Do you see where this is headed?

Tragically, in a moment of screeching brakes and flying hooves, I ruthlessly slaughtered more deer than an average Iron Range hunter fells in an entire season (one deer).

My trusty car took quite a hit, but I escaped unscathed. For once, I wasn't cursing the boat-like nature of our Buick Century.

I had gone about three years without hitting a deer, but ironically, the last deer I hit was in almost exactly the same spot on Dupont Road. That time it was the week after hunting season, and the *Hibbing Daily Tribune* had run a feature photo of two deer that survived the season basking in the sun on the side of … you guessed it, Dupont Road. The kicker read in big letters: "The Survivors."

In other words, I killed one of the survivors. Three years later, I probably killed one of her relatives.

Once, when I was driving in Iowa, a deer ran out of the corn and ran into the side of my car. Am I the Kevorkian of the deer world? Why is it that a guy who doesn't like to kill deer ends up dropping them like some kind of serial murderer? Do deer come to me for a quick release from their problem-filled lives? I hope not, because that's a job I don't want. My car insurance rates are high enough, thank you.

I just hope that at no point in my life will I depend on the mercy of deer. I can see it already. I'm caught in a bear trap out in the woods … somewhere not too far from Dupont Road. I've tried to gnaw off my own foot, but to no avail. Suddenly, deer emerge from the brush. I gaze directly into their eyes, pleading for help. The tallest deer in the center of the pack looks back without blinking. In a flash of fur and antlers, the deer stomp me with their flailing hooves while they make that screeching deer noise. EEEEEE! (stomp-stomp-stomp).

What could I say? "I didn't mean to run down your wife and daughter. I'm sorry that I left their carcasses on the side of the road." That wouldn't fly in the people world and would certainly omit me from the woodland code of brotherhood. I'll just have to avoid bear traps on my own.

Someone told me I should get one of those deer whistles for my car. I don't know. Maybe I should. I might not want to draw too much attention to my car, because I think these deer are targeting me. Perhaps a "deer laser gun" mounted on the hood would be a better option.

Wait a minute, we're trying *not* to kill the deer. Geez, this is a tough one.

I'll just make a statement to all the deer that scrounge the Sunday paper out of the Dumpster by Graysher Center and read it out by Dupont Road. First off, congratulations on your surprisingly strong reading skills. Second, and I mean this from the bottom of my heart, please do not leap out in front of my car. I do not want to kill you, and you do not want to die sprawled out on Dupont Road.

If members of the deer community are doing this intentionally, please know that there is a lot of life worth living, even for you deer. If hunting season is what worries you, then by all means, stop by our house and we'll let you lay low for a while. We've got a futon. You can bring your *Bambi* DVD if you want. There's no reason to act hastily.

OK, with that said, I'll remind my human readers to watch out for deer this time of year. They seem listless and despondent and have been taking unnecessary risks on the highways. For you hunters, you might have better luck hunting with your trucks than with your guns. You've got a lot of catching up to do if you want to match my record.

These are the Times that
Try Minnesotans' Souls

Hibbing Daily Tribune, March 2006

Do you like elaborate allegories? Try this one.

You're stuck in a room. A plate full of doughnuts sits on a table (If you don't like doughnuts picture something you do like, such as pot pies or tins of chewing tobacco). You go to grab your favorite and, suddenly, a giant bear roars into the room, eats the whole plate, and then leaves. You're not worried about the doughnuts because you just avoided a bear mauling. Even up, you figure.

Now picture the same scenario, only, instead of a bear, a squirrelly little guy named Larry wanders into the room. He starts licking the doughnuts to determine which tastes best and, after licking the whole dozen, goes back to the first one. Then he starts talking about religion and things that itch. Now you DO care about the doughnuts. And though neither the bear scenario nor Larry scenario could be described as pleasant, there is something decidedly less pleasant about Larry.

For me, January is the bear and March is Larry. March is technically "nicer," but so much more ambiguous than January. If it's warm today, it will become cold the precise moment you decide to wear a thinner jacket. In January you can count on the cold; in March you can't count on anything.

Too much convoluted symbolism? A little too *Old Man and the Sea* for your taste? Well, deal with it. March always makes me grumpy. It's a busy month, for one, but it's also so very sadistic. It gives you a taste of spring; it even gives you the first actual DAY of spring. But everyone in northern Minnesota knows that real spring won't show up for another month, and even then it might snow after stores put their swimsuits on clearance.

In March, most of the heavy duty ice begins to melt away; but when a cold snap happens, you end up with an instant sheet of very slippery ice. This led to a close call for me just last week.

You see, I claim to be a runner. To keep up this appearance, I must occasionally attempt actually running, something difficult to do when the ground is like a post-Zamboni hockey rink. Recently, I obtained these chain-like things to strap to my shoes so I could run on ice and snow. They actually work. In fact, they are pure magic. Only one problem arose: a false sense of security.

After running a brisk two miles, I jogged over the walk up to our back steps. My chest was heavy with the cold air. Without a care, I scampered over the icy walk at the base of the steps and went inside, where I removed the magic shoes.

About an hour later, I bolted out to get the papers, forgetting that I was now wearing the shoes of a mere mortal. The instant the rubber of my soles brushed the ice, I found myself in one of those "parallel with the ground contemplating what will soon be a painful fall" situations. It went about how you'd expect.

In January, you know to be careful on the ice. You know to drive slower because of all the snow. But there's March, singing its siren song, lulling us into complacency. Sure, I survived my fall. But I now greatly await a month that is exactly what it appears to be.

Here in Minnesota, that won't be until July. Maybe.

Road sign on Highway 7

From Pine Trees to Brooms:
The Present History of the Iron Range

Part Three
How Many Miles to Range Cities?

When you drive to northern Minnesota from the south on busy thoroughfares like I-35 or State Highway 53, you usually don't see the actual names of Iron Range towns on the mileage signs. Instead, you see the ambiguous phrase "Range Cities." To me, this creates a sort of mysterious, other-worldly feel to my homeland, as though an old timer stood by the side of the road bellowing: "Seventy-eight miles to the Land of Iron, Timber, and Fire, where the Gods of Steel draw their strength, and The People toil in caverns emerging only to snatch Republicans so they may feed!" Sometimes it feels like the Minnesota Department of Transportation is saying, "Range Cities: where 'those people' live." But most times I see those signs, I feel a sense of pride. I'm not from a town; I'm from a place so much bigger than one town.

Historian Pam Brunfelt argues that the Range is more than just a rural network of small towns, but actually something quite unique. "It's important to think of the Iron Range as an urban industrial corridor, that it is not a classically rural area," said Brunfelt. "Because of the fact that it is an industrial area in a geographically isolated location does not make it rural. It's still urban. If you think of the Iron Range from Coleraine to Babbitt as each town being a distinct neighborhood, then it makes sense to think of it as an urban corridor."

Brunfelt's description of the Iron Range really changed how I saw the relationship between our towns. In practice, our towns squabble quite a bit. Rivalries and parochial attitudes dominate many public meetings. I dare you to drive to Hibbing, walk into a café, and say to the retirees in attendance, "I sure am glad they moved the county fair five miles down the road to Chisholm!" They won't hurt you, not *physically,* but you will want to cry when they finish.

Like a lot of boom areas, the Iron Range developed quickly in the middle of nowhere. People and commerce happened before infrastructure. I've heard many a story that started "Before they put in *the road* …" That same road is probably still there, covered by one, maybe two layers of replacement pavement. After World War II, a few major highways bypassed some of those original roads, but for many Iron Rangers, the original roads are still tucked away in personal memory, like former lovers or near-death experiences. It might not be the kind of information that will still be around in 200 years, but on the Iron Range today, the memory of "the old days" is fresh and often the currency of most conversations. One example would be from an interview I did for this book with Heather McLaughlin, who was then director of the Hibbing Historical Society museum located in the lower level of the town's Memorial Building. (Heather scolded me for calling it the basement). I had known Heather since my first year at the *Hibbing*

Daily Tribune in 2001, so by the time I sat down for an official interview for this book, we had already discussed many of the highlights of Hibbing history, including its historic move from its old location to one three miles to the south. The repetitive nature of the stories created a lot of exchanges like this one:

> Aaron Brown: What makes Hibbing's history different from your average Range town?
>
> Heather McLauglin: I don't know. I'm not really sure why Hibbing is more interesting.
>
> AB: Is it because Hibbing moved? Did that create an attitude in town?
>
> HM: That's one of the big things, but Hibbing is different in a lot more ways than that. If you want to talk about the move just ask me about the move.
>
> AB: Tell me about the move. Tell me like I was a tourist from Iowa.
>
> HM: I don't talk to them.

Heather is another modern Iron Ranger, a third generation Hibbing native who grew disinterested in her computer career training. She used her degree to get the job of archiving and somehow explaining the story of the Iron Range's largest city to the world at large. She and the historical society published a book of historical photographs called *Hibbing, Minnesota* that gives readers a strong impression of the town's development. During our conversation, I asked Heather to list what she would consider to be the "greatest hits" of Hibbing and Iron Range history. She would know. She's scoured the archives and has a working knowledge of Range history you normally don't see from people as young as Heather. She spent years archiving the historical society's pictures and records, but you'll find a lot more than just papers and pictures in the museum. A full scale model of "old Hibbing" sprawls across the back wall, showing the time before the bustling town was moved three miles south in the 1920s. Household items used by early city residents are found throughout the museum such as chairs, kitchen utensils, and the equipment that early miners were required to purchase and maintain out of their own pockets. Modern history on the Iron Range only goes back about 110 years. At the time I write this, there are people in Hibbing who could walk into that museum and say, "Hey, that's dad's old chair" or "I think I sold that at a rummage sale two summers ago." Such is the nature of a young old town like Hibbing. These are the things that Heather and I talked about.

Reluctantly, she did list her "Greatest Hits of Hibbing History." First, the strikes of 1907 and 1916 that I already mentioned. Also, Hibbing's move, when the whole city was moved on rolling logs from one location to another. In exchange, the city received the nation's most expensive school and one of the most expensive small town city halls built at the time. Then there were the men who helped make that deal possible: Victor Power, and his brothers. This Power dynasty shaped the entire attitude about how cities dealt with mining companies during and after the strikes. But two other stories stand out, both largely unknown and both examples of the strange nature of early Iron Range culture. They are the stories of Black Jack Webb and the Duel of 1910.

Heather McLaughlin described the Black Jack Webb story to me:

Black Jack Webb, 1914

"John 'Black Jack' Webb had, I think, seven children, ranging in age from seventeen down to six or something like that. He lived out in Kitzville, but he had hunting shacks all over the place.

"One of the boys, his oldest, came into town and reported to the police that his father had been molesting the youngest daughter. Now, nobody knows if that's true or not because when the police sent out a posse to get him, he shot and killed three police officers: Cort, Hayes, and Cassidy. The rest scrambled, and he took off, and he was running around between his shacks for a couple of weeks. They had this huge manhunt. It was the biggest manhunt ever in the state of Minnesota at that time.

"This woman in Chisholm saw him raiding her garden. He made a motion for her to be quiet and then took off into the woods. She called the cops, and they found him in one of his shacks. As they approached the building, there were gunshots, and he killed himself. Before he shot himself, he had scribbled notes to his children to stay away from the drink, don't end up like me. I've got copies of the notes he wrote to his kids. It's really kind of sad.

"They took his body and they tied it over the right front fender of the police car, like a deer. They were all hanging off the car, and they drove through downtown Hibbing a hootin' and a hollerin'. Yeah, that wouldn't fly today. They were very happy to have him dead. I've got a picture of that…his actual body tied to the car."

In the context of today's stories of violent episodes, you can't help but wonder what day-to-day life was like in this past, but not too far past, era on the Iron Range.

The Duel of 1910

Meantime, in a display case somewhere in the middle of Hibbing Historical Society Museum, visitors will see two pistols with a remarkable story. An article in the October 29, 1910 edition of the *Hibbing Daily Tribune* explains where they came from. The series of cascading headlines are reprinted here:

"REVOLVER DUEL
ONE MAN KILLED

"Sam Kacich Kills Pete Radovich in Battle with Guns as Result of Quarrel – Came to the Village Yesterday Afternoon and Bought Weapons.

"Appeared Friendly in Store and Ate Together – On Way Home the Quarrel was Resumed and Homicide Resulted – Kacich is Arraigned Today.

"One man dead and the other suffering from a broken arm is the result of a duel fought last evening between two Montenegrins."

In summary, on Friday, October 28, 1910, Pete Radovich fired three shots at his friend Sam Kacich, wounding him in the elbow. Kacich then shot Radovich in the head at close range, killing him instantly. This exchange was part of a premeditated duel between the two miners, who worked at the nearby Leetonia Mine.

This didn't happen in Tombstone, Deadwood, or Dodge City. This duel, the only known duel in the state of Minnesota, took place on the streets of Hibbing, a short distance from the police station. Kacich was never convicted of murder because a skillful young defense attorney successfully argued a plea of self defense. The other guy was indeed trying to kill Sam, argued attorney Vic Power who would later become the most influential mayor in Iron Range history.

No one knows what their argument was about. Common arguments of the time varied, but didn't stray far from certain themes. In 1910, men outnumbered women by scores, so most men went home, well, lets say "disappointed" on Saturday nights, usually to boarding houses filled with other "disappointed" men. Historically, this sort of climate leads either to violence or the creation of garage rock bands. Tragically, the men of the early Range had no garages or guitars. They had dances and liquor, and if the combination of the two did not favor them, they had fighting and the prospect of more work in the mine shaft early the next day.

Then there were unions. The first great Iron Range miners' strike of 1907 had failed just three years before Sam and Pete's argument. Then again, the argument could have been politics. Many residents of Hibbing couldn't vote because of their immigrant status. When they could, mine bosses adopted a practice of having their employees vote on the job site, with a foreman looking over their shoulder. That's why most Iron Range politicians of the early part of the 20th century were Republicans well connected with the business community and openly disdainful of labor unions. Working men often disagreed about what was really best for them.

But no one knows why Sam Kacich and Pete Radovich decided to try to kill each other in 1910. Whatever caused it, sometime in the evening, the two men decided they would participate in a traditional duel to the death. According to the newspaper article, the men were known to be good friends. Both from Montenegro, they reached a formal agreement by which the winner of the duel would receive the loser's lands in the old country.

To fully appreciate the insanity of this duel, you have to know a little about how old Hibbing was laid out. These men lived in Leetonia location, a little cluster of houses next to an underground mine of the same name. Since almost everyone had to walk in those days, getting from Leetonia to the big city of Hibbing, about two miles, was not as easy as it is today. You had to hoof it. So these guys, probably after a long day of working, got into some sort of argument. Their first stop was at Cohen's store in the Power Theatre block in downtown Hibbing. According to the *Tribune*, Kacich bought two .38 caliber revolvers along with two pounds of grapes. Kacich and Radovich proceeded to eat the grapes in the store. The store clerk reported that the two were very friendly to each other, even though they said they were going to duel. I imagine he thought it was a joke. Even in 1910, the concept of dueling must have seemed passé, kind of like dancing the Charleston for my generation. At that time in Range history, however, I bet the sale of two revolvers in one shift was a good night for the clerk. So sell them he did.

Anecdotes I've heard had the two men visiting saloons as they traveled down Third Avenue, at each place talking about their upcoming demise. It was presumably along this tour that they devised their plan for the winner to receive the loser's land in Montenegro. At some point, the merriment ended and they went about their grim task.

Off they went, back to Leetonia. Later testimony showed that the men decided not to walk all the way home. The police and morgue, after all, were in Hibbing. So, they began the duel in the viaduct about four blocks from Third Avenue, the road home. There were no first hand witnesses, only the testimony of Kacich. According to the *Tribune* again, the two men drew their weapons by the railroad tracks and began firing. Radovich shot three times, hitting Kacich once and shattering his elbow. Kacich then fired one shot through the roof of Radovich's mouth and into his head. They were standing at such close range, probably only four or five feet apart, that gun powder burned Radovich's face. He died instantly.

According to the paper, a switchman heard the shots. William Kruper, coming up the railroad tracks into town, found Radovich's body and notified police, just three blocks away. Meantime, Kacich had trudged back into town and holed up at a saloon. Dejected, he told the bartender what had happened and requested to be brought to the jail. In a short time, an officer came to collect Kacich, and the legal process began. The last paragraph of the newspaper account read like this:

"Kacich expressed regret that he was not killed by one of the bullets and his demeanor is one of abject dejection though he has a strong plea to make at the coming trial. Self defense will of course be the grounds for the homicide."

In a college journalism class, I recall hearing the phrase, "Newspapers write the first draft of history." Whatever newspapers print shows a lot about the people served by that newspaper. Today, self defense seems a long shot defense for someone who participates in a duel. At the very least, manslaughter seems to be a no-brainer. But in 1910, the self defense plea seemed reasonable to the writer of the newspaper article. No one stands down from a duel, and if you're in a duel, it'd be just foolish not to return fire.

This duel marked the end of the pioneer stage of Hibbing and the Minnesota iron ranges. The early history of Hibbing is a story of labor fights, immigrant strife, and the unbreakable power of the mining companies. But a few years after the duel, the labor movement scored a draw in the great strike of 1916, which was the beginning of a long shift that led to monumental victories during the Franklin Roosevelt administration and finally after World War II, when labor victories began to create the modern sense that a mining job was a "good job." Shortly after the duel, Victor Power, the same lawyer who sprung Kacich from jail on a plea of self defense, scored victory after victory against the mining companies and built the infrastructure of modern Hibbing. He could well have ended up in the governor's office if it weren't for his unexpected death in 1926.

We don't have duels on the streets of Range towns anymore. Gunplay still occurs from time to time, but it's usually related to drugs or domestic strife, and there is no honor or reprieve for the shooters. Our turmoil, our frustrations, and our anger play out in different, much more subtle ways now. Thus the records are not as clear or compelling as the accounts of the Kacich/Radovich duel of 1910.

So when you're in Hibbing, stop down in the baseme … er … lower level of the Memorial Building on 23rd St. and 4th Ave. Take a look at those pistols and other memorabilia, and think about how things were and how things are. 100 years is a blink of God's eye,

but look how far we have come. Let's have some grapes and talk
this over.

Cherry Reds

My hometown of Cherry, Minnesota, was a home to, if not a shared birthplace, of the modern American labor, socialist, and communist movements. They also had a pretty good football team. I've dabbled in all of the above.

I have to stress the word "dabble." We may be more than half a century removed from Joe McCarthy and the red baiting of the 1950s, but the majority of Americans still don't feel a lot of warm fuzzies for commies. That's why I feel compelled to say that I am not now nor have I ever been a member of the Communist Party. But I do feel a sense of pride in our hometown's communist roots, kind of how Great Plains residents might feel about the pioneers who broke the sod where their houses now stand. Sure, those pioneers didn't deal fairly with the Indians and were often crushingly racist, but in the context of their time, they achieved amazing things. Communism today is associated with dictators and human rights violations, so I want to be clear that the communists of Cherry did business in a different time and with different means. My personal politics are, generally speaking, a more centrist shade of liberalism, but I can't help but feel a spark of agreement when I read about the goals of those original Cherry communists, all of which came to pass or remain mainstream campaign issues: the right of workers to organize, health care access for all, human rights, equal justice under the law, and proper conditions for all working men and women.

The original Cherry Reds were, by and large, first generation Finnish immigrants. Many Finns left their country because of working conditions back home and often developed socialist views as a result. Thus, there was a stereotype that all the Finns coming to northern Minnesota were rabble rousers. In the early 1900s, Finns were blacklisted from working in the mines because owners feared they would organize unions. Many Finns turned to farming, settling in places like Floodwood, Toivola, Meadowlands, Sax, Zim, and, naturally, Cherry.

According to legend, Cherry got its name from a Finnish immigrant who tried to grow cherry trees in our cold weather climate. The postmaster was amused by the story so he named the mail outpost "Cherry." Having grown up in that area in the 1980s, I can still remember the co-op grocery store, which is now a salvage yard. A cooperative recreation park called Mesaba Co-op Park is still functional, built mostly by socialists in 1930. It maintains a strong membership and hosts liberal political functions and camps, even though the communists stopped coming decades ago.

The reputation of communism in Cherry spread beyond Minnesota and still crops up when I tell people where I'm from. Bestselling author John Sandford used an Iron Range communist subplot in his serial thriller *Hidden Prey*. Actually, I've come across too many veiled references to Iron Range communists in political novels for it to be coincidental. Though Cherry is no longer a communist hotbed, and the township reliably votes for liberal candidates. Al Gore beat George W. Bush by about thirty points in Cherry; four years later John Kerry won by forty points. Finnish heritage is still strong, though it weakens a bit with each generation. When I grew up in nearby McDavitt Township, many local surnames ended in the Finnish –ala, -anen, or –I, with consecutive kk's and nn's spliced in the middle. The old trophies in the case at the high school match the names you see on mailboxes when you drive through the network of dirt roads that crisscross the township. The owners of those mailboxes often visit those trophies, if not in person, then in memory.

Before those trophies were won, back when those roads were first being cut through woods and fields of what is now Cherry, the Halberg family was talking, in Finnish and later in English, about workers' rights. They joined the Industrial Workers of the World. They organized. Their son Arvo paid special attention.

Just as every town has a reputation, every town also has a famous son or daughter. In Cherry, our famous son is Arvo Halberg, who later became known as Gus Hall. Even in the time I was growing up, Hall wasn't quite the household name he was in the 1950s, '60s, and '70s. Gus Hall was the chairman of the Communist Party USA, and was for decades the highest ranking and most prominent communist in the United States. He came from an era when the labor and social justice movement was just starting to see success, a time before organized labor was distancing itself from socialism. Gus Hall is most remembered as a famous communist, but he was also a founding organizer of the United Steelworkers of America. The USWA is still the largest union on the Iron Range, and local labor officials, even former Gov. Rudy Perpich, were well acquainted with the Halberg family.

Hall's 1930s organizational tactics, picked up during training in the Soviet Union, were hardly "Minnesota Nice." He had to clear up several misdemeanors before he could serve in the Navy during World War II. Later a four-time presidential candidate, Hall spent eight years in Leavenworth during McCarthyism for violating the Smith Act, an anti-communist law that was later deemed unconstitutional.

In 1999, my friend Andy Miller and I were the last reporters to interview Gus Hall before his death the next year at the age of ninety.

Early in 1999, I was asked to start up a community newspaper for a group of small townships using a grant. A local woman who was a prolific grant writer had somehow written and received a grant to start a newspaper without a tremendous expectation of actually receiving the money.

"I don't know how to run a newspaper," she said.

I was the one who was supposed to create and produce the first three editions of this community newspaper. After that, someone else from the community was supposed to take over. No one ever did, so the *Cherry Community Dispatch* had only a summer fling with the reading public. I wanted to do a three-part series on famous people from Cherry, all based on the assumption that we could find three famous people from Cherry. Gus Hall was the anchor. I found another guy, Bob Pappas, who adapted the first version of the arcade game "Frogger" for home computer audiences in the 1980s, just a short time after he left Cherry High School. My third guy was a baseball pitcher named Eric Goerdt who had just led the Cherry baseball team to its first and only state title and was being scouted by the Major Leagues. It helped that he and my friend Andy carpooled to Madison together. Though he never did make a splash in pro baseball, I hope our front page story provides him some opportunity to reminisce in his later years.

As the single most famous Cherry resident, Gus Hall's interview was key to the series. So, how does one contact the General Secretary of the Communist Party USA? Here is the step-by-step procedure we used. 1) Call the number on the communist website. 2) Ask for the General Secretary. 3) Talk to the General Secretary. Actually, Gus Hall didn't answer the phone the first time I called, but he did answer subsequent calls to the main number. His assistant, who answered first, was a woman named Carole Marks, which sounds like "Marx" on the phone. "No relation" she told me, as I'm sure she told everyone.

We set up a time to interview Hall by phone from the principal's office of Cherry High School to the Manhattan headquarters of the CPUSA. Andy and I conducted the interview together, partly because we were both interested and partly because it seemed smart to have someone to back up the story should anyone question why the communist headquarters appeared on the school's long distance phone records.

The interview lasted about fifteen minutes. Hall was then eighty-nine and in declining health. Mostly, we asked about stories, perspective from the early years of labor organizing. Better journalists might have pressed him harder on why he remained so loyal to the party and the Soviet Union after the fall of communism in most of the world. To tell the truth, we didn't have the heart. This was one of Hall's few interviews with an independent newspaper outside of the CPUSA's own *People's Weekly World* and would prove to be the last interview of his life. He just seemed to be happy telling the stories of how he and his dad helped build the Mesaba Co-Op Park and how his upbringing shaped his views.

We mailed a copy of the story to the communists in New York. I got an e-mail from Carole Marks saying that our feature was the "best coverage (the CPUSA) had ever received in its history." That's when I had my first inkling that we had gone easy on the communists. They asked to reprint the stories in *People's Weekly World*. Andy and I agreed, amazed at what we had wandered into. And so that's why today our names still appear as contributing writers in the archives of the *People's Weekly World*, a fact that may well keep me out of some of our nation's high standing clubs and organizations, such as the government.

About a year later, Gus Hall died. Andy received an invitation to his funeral in New York. I was quoted in a couple of news stories having been the last reporter to interview Hall. Most of the news coverage portrayed Hall as the last remnant of the communist party in America. A guest column in the conservative *National Review* by Ronald Radosh (Oct. 20, 2000) rebuked Hall, especially for his condoning of Stalin's crimes and tactics and the hypocrisy of his Soviet-financed wealthy lifestyle as the self-declared leader of the working class. Indeed, Hall was not everything he claimed to be, though for the many shortcomings detailed in Radosh's column, Hall was sincere in his ideology and liked by those who knew him personally. According to the reports and stories we heard, Hall was a big man, jovial, and quick with a story that involved his past. He often dressed like a banker and took joy in telling unsuspecting conversationalists that he was actually a leader in the Communist Party. As each Soviet satellite nation fell to popular forces, and even as Soviet Russia expunged its communist government, Hall told everyone who asked that he still believed socialism would come to the world. He repeated this to Andy and me in our phone interview, the same quiet, tired way other old men would remark on a coming rain. "Looks like a storm comin.' Workers of the world gonna' unite, I 'spose."

All things end eventually. I think I mentioned that, while Cherry was known most for communism, it was known second for football. For many years, Cherry produced conference winning football teams, despite its small population. For a couple years in junior high, I was a lineman for the Tigers. On paper, I was going to grow into an all-state lineman. In practice, however, my lack of hand-eye coordination relegated me to newspaper work. Mercifully, I ended my brief football career after junior high. I bring it up only because the early promise of my football skills reminds me of the early promise of communism, the promise that the people of Cherry had embraced so fully at the time. So as a young writer, coming of age in Cherry, I felt a kinship with the communist Gus Hall and his ideas even if time, and facts, rubbed off the gilding.

From Cherry came the Steelworkers, and the communists. The former are the reason the Iron Range's top export in the 1950s, '60s, and '70s was not iron ore, but young, college-educated professionals who made modern America. The latter, well, there was a bit of trouble in eastern Europe. You're welcome and we're sorry, respectively.

Communism failed, certainly in its intended form. Still, to the end, Gus Hall maintained his belief in socialism. He was cast as a relic of another time, though he played a role in history and left a mark on the place where I'm from. When you drive through Cherry on State Highway 37, you'll notice it's still a farming area with an active dairy farm and many hayfields on the main highway and back roads. Many of the current farmers are direct descendants of those Red Finns blacklisted from the mines for organizing, though the generations of daily farm chores has altered the current generation's political beliefs just a touch. You'll still see a sign advertising Mesaba Co-op Park. You'll notice the school, which was also built by early residents, and it, along with the notion that everyone deserves a quality public education, remains the center of the community. Whatever success and comfort I ever know will come from what I learned in that building.

Yes, communism failed and caused unrest across the globe. But there's still something to extract from the spirit of the Red Finns. Here in Cherry, where Gus Hall and I are from, we still believe in the good that comes from working hard and working together. If we can keep that idea separate from the Gulags and the loss of human rights and freedoms, we've really got something.

We'll get it right eventually. Meantime, my memories remain the same. The dirt roads of my childhood will always lead to old farm houses where secrets once occurred, where working people fought for their rights attracting the nervous glances of a nation that feared the color red. Cherry red.

Ethnic Lines Blur

In 100 years, immigrants from forty-three different countries came to the Iron Range. As recently as 1985, when I reported to first grade at Forbes Elementary, teachers still asked their students "What are you?" Despite our exposure to *Sesame Street* most still knew to respond "Italian!" "Slovenian!" "Finn!" "Irish!" I always struggled with the question since I am no more than a quarter of anything and a little bit of everything. But I tried. Quarter Finn, Eighth Norwegian, Eighth Swede, and the rest a convoluted mix of English, French, German, Dutch, and Irish Protestant. The Browns were Cornish miners who emigrated to work the underground shafts, weaving their way along iron formations through Canada, Michigan's upper peninsula, and eventually the Mesabi, Vermilion, and Cuyana Iron Ranges. Along the way, they married Scandinavian women until I came along, looking the way you'd expect a NorFinnSwede to look, with England's most common last name. I don't point myself out because I'm special, but because there's thousands of us shuffling around these woods, self-identified Iron Rangers just a few degrees separated from most of Europe.

"I don't think (ethnic heritage) is what defines Iron Rangers any more anyway," said Pam Brunfelt. "I think television has had a huge impact on that. I think more of what identifies an Iron Ranger today is a lifestyle that is tied to the land and tied to family.

There's intense loyalty to family ties that you don't see everywhere else. Iron Range families have not tended to move on. They have set down very deep roots. Children, though they may have gone to the [Minneapolis-St. Paul area] and made new lives, still pretty much identify themselves with this place. I don't think you can say that about other places in the State of Minnesota."

As of 2005, humans removed more than 4,278,562,000 tons of iron ore and taconite from the Iron Range over our 125 year history, mostly from the Mesabi. That's heavy. This ore provided seventy-five percent of the steel used by the United States in World War II and vast portions of our nation's infrastructure and manufactured goods over the past century. Today, even though production levels are smaller, Iron Range ore trades on the international market and aids or influences steel production in the fast-growing nations of China, India, and the many industrial regions of South America and Europe. Large parts of Iron Range culture endure, but our fate is now intertwined with the global economy and the growth of nations on the other side of the globe. The Iron Range location closest to the industrial giants who master our mines is no longer on the east Range, closest to Cleveland, Pittsburgh, and New York, but at the bottom of our deepest abandoned mine shaft at Soudan. If it weren't for all the lava, miners could just keep digging there to meet our new bosses in India, China, and Japan.

So much for history. Now what? Pine trees or brooms?

A Letter to My Son

Hibbing Daily Tribune, June 2005

Dear Henry,

You were born at 6:47 p.m. on Thursday, May 26 at the Fairview University Medical Center-Mesabi in Hibbing. I know that's a lot of information all at once, but you have to understand that grownups like long names for things, especially when they include hyphens.

It was a long ordeal getting you into this world. First, your mom's nine months of pregnancy challenged us. (Why all the kicking and dropping, eh?). Then, when it was time for you to show up, Mom had to endure a long labor before doctors delivered you by c-section instead. You weighed nine pounds, eleven ounces and, by the look of things, inherited the dominant "Giant Brown Family Head" gene. Luckily, you were cute enough for your mom not to hold this against you.

Spending so much time in the hospital gave me the opportunity to think. I write this knowing that you can't read yet. We'll work on that. And we'll work on holding your head up and feeding yourself, too. I just wanted to put a few thoughts down before we took you home from the hospital, because life is going to get pretty crazy over the next few days, or eighteen years from what I'm told.

It can be cold here. You might have picked up on that when we showed up at the hospital in gale force winds and chilly rain. Fortunately, you were born in the summertime. Yes, this is summer in your home state. We'll try our best to keep you warm. If experience has taught me anything, it's that the best clothes to keep you warm are also the dumbest looking. Keep this in mind when we dress you up in some of the outfits we have waiting for you. Also, keep in mind that the warmest feelings come from the people who will be your friends even when you're wearing dumb looking clothes.

It can be confusing here. I know, because I've been here twenty-five years and still don't know what the hell is going on. Oh, yeah. Don't say "hell." You'll note that at this point, I still have some parenting skills to work on. I'm hoping that by the time you can read, you appreciate irony. Perhaps by then, I'll have learned to say "phooey" when I can't easily put together a simple item, such as a cradle, instead of that particularly nasty word I used a few weeks ago. I also hope that you always try to find the answers before giving up on this confusing world. I further hope that your cradle does not collapse with you in it.

It can be complicated here. I can't promise you that everything is going to be perfect. You will love and lose, experience heartbreak and deception. But you will know happiness if you don't let these things control your life. You will also see sunrises over the lake, meet all your grandparents, learn how to write, paint, play, and fish, and look out over a world full of even more possibilities than existed when I was your age.

As I look at you in your crib, not knowing what interests you will develop and what course your life will take, I realize that all the things they say about being a father are true. I'm already proud of you. I already feel joy in my heart just thinking about you. I already love you. And if you don't hear it enough when you're old enough to read, let this letter remind you that I always will.

Love,

Dad

Douglas and George Brown

Room for Two

Hibbing Daily Tribune, July 2007

On July 2, we welcomed twin boys into our world. Douglas and George join our son Henry in what now becomes a pretty big brood by modern standards. I used to look at those families – the ones with waves of sticky toddlers teeming out of shopping carts and restaurant booths – and wonder how *that* happened. Now I know.

My wife Christina and I have expected these guys for a long time. We found out early after a scare brought us to the hospital. On the ultrasound screen, where we desperately hoped to see one healthy baby, we saw two healthy babies. We entered a trance; overwhelmed with joy, trepidation, and rough estimates of diaper prices. But for all the months of waiting, the whole idea seemed conceptual (no pun intended), like an album cover design drawn on a bar napkin.

Now, after a couple months of bed rest, a tanker truck of ice cream, and frequent requisitions from fast food restaurants, Doug and George are here. They were born a couple weeks early, but healthy, hungry, and loud. I've had plenty of "wow" moments in my life, but no wow compares to holding these guys in the nursery and realizing that both would be coming home with us.

There are so many fears involved in parenting. These fears range from the big stuff, like health and safety, to the fear of somehow screwing up your kids by feeding them too many hot dogs or artificial sweetener. In red state households: "What if my kids don't like sports?" In blue state households: "What if my kids lack whimsy and advanced test scores?" For me, the biggest fear with the twins was that I would mix them up. I've known lots of twins, and invariably, I think Bob is Bill and Bill is Bob. That's fine when Bill works at the gas station and Bob is the mail carrier, but you can't get away with that when the twins live across the hall and share your DNA.

On the big day, though, these fears melted away. There's no mistaking Doug – who on his birthday looked a little like my dad, but mostly like himself. And George resembles Henry a little, but a good look into his eyes shows you that he's his own baby. Each has a unique personality, even if their activities are now limited to three or four predominantly biological tasks. As a writer, it hit me that our boys are all new characters – vibrant, with virtues and flaws, but ultimately deep and distinct. I don't know the men they'll come to be yet, but I so look forward to the adventure of finding out.

I won't sugar coat it. These first nights are totally kicking our butts. But even though I didn't know it all those months ago, there is room for two more at our table and in our hearts. Most of our fears have proven unfounded, with the exception of diaper prices (These guys go through Huggies the way an old time newspaper reporter goes through unfiltered cigarettes). Doug and George, welcome to Earth in general and our house in particular. You're the sixth generation of Browns on the Iron Range, and who knows what the future will bring? We'll keep things interesting for you, and I'm sure you'll keep it interesting for us.

After all, we're one of *those* families now: big, sticky, and loud.

Talkin' Baby Talk Blues

Hibbing Daily Tribune, September 2007

Your job often defines how people see you. My dad has worked as a mechanic and in building maintenance for decades. Therefore, when something breaks at a family event, he is the one asked to put down his plate of holiday food to unclog pipes, tighten bolts, or check belts. No one ever asks me. I once saw a relative ask a dentist to look at a tooth as the dentist walked past his yard. Again, not something I am asked to do.

I'm a writer and college speech instructor. That means people ask me to write pro bono press releases or "say something" at most social functions. That's OK. I'm glad to help, and it's harder for me not to talk than it is for me to talk. But lately, I can't help but feel a bit like a poser. After all, I'm supposed to articulate important thoughts on paper and teach others the finer points of communication, but I live in a house where I can be overheard saying: "Do you need to poop? ... oh, yes, that's a tree ... oh, you mean you're hungry. Never mind."

For those scoring at home, we have three kids: a two-year-old boy and twin boys born this past summer. Life with three kids creates many interesting communication challenges that never seem to find their way into any college speech curriculum.

I've already noticed one thing about having three kids compared to just one. Instant street cred. Sure, I know a lot of people have three or more kids, and that the actual act of producing three children is as easy as, well, you know. But three is the magic number where child superiorists leave you alone (Child superiorists: my new word to describe people who use the developmental progress of their multiple children as a blunt weapon against your eardrums).

But as proud we are to have survived our time as "parents of three" (as of press time, anyway) we still struggle to understand the little humans who live in our house.

Henry, our oldest, is a big fan of heavy equipment. Trucks, bulldozers, and back hoes all enjoy special affection. Of course, to him, they are twucks, boo-dozas, and bag-os. Henry's favorite verb is "play." So we often hear the H-man say things like, "Pway twuck?" or his recent favorite, "pway bag-o?"

Now if you heard someone say "pway bag-o," you probably wouldn't think he was asking you to hold a toy digger while he operated the boom. You might think he was saying "Free bagel?" to which someone might say, "No! Bagels cost money!" It takes a lot of trial and error to learn the true meaning of "pway bag-o." This can be quite frustrating, both for the adults who try to understand and encourage their kid, and the kid who desperately wants to move sand with his bag-o.

It'd be a lot easier for us if the babies spoke the same language, but they still rely entirely on nonverbal signals. "Waaa," for "I'm hungry." "Waaaaaaa," for "I'm hungry and wet." "Waaaaaaa, URP, blech, waaaaaa …. Mmmm" for "I was feeling kind of bloated but then I barfed on you, and now I feel much better. Oh, look, is that a moving object? Jolly good!"

Soon enough, these boys will speak like grown-ups, perhaps even flex their rhetorical muscles to achieve objectives. By then, I'll be no use to them. I'll have emptied my brain of everything I learned in college to make room for a language of goos, gaas, and the abbreviated names of heavy equipment. Play bag-o, anyone?

Local Child Raised
by Monkeys and Talking Trains

Hibbing Daily Tribune, April 2007

I've learned that when you tell parenting stories, you need to distance yourself from claiming any sort of expertise. It's a little like advertising for mutual funds; past performance is not indicative of future results.

I say this because if you had talked to me eight months ago, I might have told you – OK, bragged – that our son Henry didn't show much interest in TV. He would watch a few minutes here and there but spent more time playing with blocks or trucks. I might have assumed that the logical progression from this would have been for Henry to eschew TV entirely, build a perpetual motion machine by age five, and staff our household with fully-functional, non-evil robot servants before he hit junior high.

This was, of course, before he saw his first *Thomas the Tank Engine* video and got hooked on his four o'clock *Curious George* fix. Naturally, both programs have book and toy counterparts. Now we see more trains and monkeys than an Amtrak conductor on *Planet of the Apes*.

Thomas the Tank Engine has been around a long time. I remember when Ringo Starr was the "conductor" who told stories of the cavalcade of self-aware, adventure-prone trains on the fictional Island of Sodor. In the years since, both Alec Baldwin and George Carlin have narrated Thomas stories. I'm pretty sure this is the only thing Ringo Starr, Alec Baldwin, and George Carlin have in common. (If you want to blow your mind, watch George Carlin narrate a Thomas story and then put on his comedy album with the "Seven Words You Can't Say on Television.")

Thematically, the best "Thomas" video we've seen is "Races, Rescues, and Runaways" (one of the Baldwin videos). This video features a series of adventures in which trains, blinded by pride or power, attempt to do things they shouldn't with disastrous results. Trains derail, crash into box cars full of jam, and burst into buildings full of people. Outside of Sodor, their actions would cause a near endless string of drug and alcohol tests for their plastic human crews. In the videos, however, humans show a glib, almost nonchalant attitude toward these rail yard debacles. If real life rules applied, several of these yard workers would be splayed out on tracks while Poindexter the Ambulance (TM) went looking for salvageable limbs.

The video ends with a musical montage recapping the very best of the rail disasters set to a tune called "Accidents Happen." I haven't been able to locate the exact lyrics to this song, but to my ear one of the refrains goes, "Accidents happen now and again, people and trains get smashed." This reminds me of a story an ex-railroader told me about a northern Minnesota town where, when the train slowed to pass through, the railroad crew would jump off the train, run to a nearby liquor store, and run back to the accelerating train with beer. Indeed, people and trains DO get smashed (I've been assured that stories like these are part of a bygone era of railroading, which has since seen massive safety improvements ... except in Sodor).

I haven't analyzed *Curious George* much here. I won't have enough space to explore the complex relationship between a bachelor who lives in the city and wears yellow safari clothes every day, and his monkey, who in real life would be on the ten o'clock news every night.

I'm still glad that Henry likes these programs instead of *Barney,* the *Wiggles,* and the *Teletubbies* (all horror shows for adults). We may have TV in our lives, which might possibly prevent Henry from getting his Ph.D. by age twenty. But I am glad to have learned so much about the travails of jaunty little trains and a monkey who often breaks the law in a very, very cute way. The parenting train just keeps on choogling along.

A Kerry/Edwards rally at the Hibbing Memorial Building in 2004

Rocks Populi

The Iron Range is known first for its mines and historically sketchy economy. Second, people know about our hockey, as our teams often abuse metropolitan area squads in the state tournament. If the Iron Range gets any further recognition, it is for our tradition of labor and political organization. Those who disembark on the Iron Range for the first time might not notice the political significance of the place, especially in an odd numbered year. In fact, those passing any given Range town on the highway might wonder why the people who live in those red-stained houses with shovels and scrap wood piled in the back have such importance in deciding who is elected to the governor's mansion or Congress in this state. But those who become acquainted with Minnesota politics gradually begin to realize that the place is a strange electoral phenomenon, like a quasar or the Big Green Monster of Boston's Fenway Park. Not necessarily liberal, though considered by some to be socialistic. Not necessarily conservative, though sometimes criticized as backward and parochial. The Iron Range political tradition is proud, loud, and takes some getting used to, even for those holding the most elite degrees in political science.

Those of us who grew up here weren't taught that we were radical. We were taught that people from the Twin Cities, probably wearing suits, were coming to get us, and that we needed to be prepared to defend ourselves, probably with guns. Riots were discouraged but regarded as occasionally necessary. I also know people who taught their kids labor movement folk songs, which isn't what you see in the suburbs. But regardless of our parents' personal politics, Iron Rangers learned that people from other places were gunning for you.

To be sure, some forces in the world seem to be "out to get" the kind of working class communities you find on the Iron Range. But even my limited experience on this planet has taught me that not ALL people from outside the Iron Range are trying to buy out our property and make our grandmas eat dog food instead of sarmas. But that's the primal urge screaming in the political consciousness of most Iron Range voters.

Largely because of its 120-year connection to valuable stores of rich iron ore, thick forests of pine, immigration, and all the resulting conflict over jobs and resources, the Iron Range pulses with politics. Politics is just a sophisticated way of solving the "scarce resource" conflicts cavemen once addressed with clubs. Sometimes, local politics is better than the brutal, public clubbing of a hairy, half-naked caveman. But if it ever does resemble such a thing, the reason is simple: tradition.

Iron Range politics of today center on tradition. On a good day, we fill with pride thinking of all the progress our ancestors and our leaders have brought us over the years. It's true; the result of our bruising, but bold, political tradition has been a remarkably resilient society and infrastructure that has long outlived similar mining economies around the country. On a bad day, however, our tradition serves only to mask mediocrity, cronyism, and aversion to change. As the population declines, so too does the pool of new ideas and new leaders.

As I have often said, the Range is not particularly "old" as a region. Only about a century, often less, separates most Iron Range families from the time their ancestors moved here. But the tumultuous first few decades created a mystique about the place that has since been dubbed "tradition" by those who have filled the big shoes of early labor and political innovators. Since then, our population has aged with the landscape, and we are no longer a bustling place of young immigrants with simple but great ambitions of upward mobility and fairness. The net result of this tradition is a narrative of conventional wisdom, part good and part bad. This narrative is now widely known around Minnesota and in national political circles. It is this:

The Iron Range elects Democrat-Farmer-Laborites (we don't have a Democratic Party in Minnesota, we have the DFL). The last Republican elected in the heart of the Iron Range won during the Eisenhower 1950s, before the state legislature was considered "partisan," and all the party politics were done through winking, drinking, and coalition-building. Since then, the Iron Range has elected Democrats as reliably as the orbit of the moon. There are Republicans around. They vote and run for office, but they always lose because *the Iron Range elects Democrat-Farmer-Laborites*. The Iron Range elects DFLers no matter what they look like. We like our politicians large and purple, with a meaty grip and the letters D-F-L next to their name in the paper.

At their worst, Iron Range politicians are crooked assholes. In this regard, not much is different here than anywhere else. But conversely, Iron Range politicians, at their best, are honest assholes: or at least act that way to achieve their objectives. In Range politics, we don't have any Gary Coopers. We only have

John Waynes, but they don't look as good, they talk funny, and their last names are usually ninety-five percent consonants.

There are indeed many "nice" public servants on the Iron Range, but most of them dwell with relative obscurity in a mushy middle, occasionally renaming schools, funding sewer plants, or passing bills cleaning up language in education codes. Our most historic public figures, however, were leaders with a reputation of strong-arming their way to legislative and electoral success, creating enemies and never forgetting who those enemies were – ever. In short, Iron Range voters reward "tough" the way most other voters reward "smooth."

That's the conventional wisdom. Is it true? In part, yes. But the complete truth is decidedly more complex.

The Range, where "poli sci" sounds like some kind of ethnic dish

Anyone who follows modern politics is loaded to the gills with conventional political stereotypes applied to the United States of the early twenty-first century. "Red," or conservative, states or regions are rural, evangelical Christian places where people love guns, the unborn, and NASCAR. People in these places hate hippies, homosexuality, and high-minded professor types. "Blue," or liberal, states or regions support government programs, "anything goes" social policies, fancy fair trade coffees, and all remaining genres of folk music. Their people hate idiotic rednecks, American flag bandanas, and sometimes meat.

If you look at our voting trends, the Iron Range seems to be a "blue" region, a reliable Democratic portion of a blue-leaning state. But our numbers hide a secret: All of the descriptions I use for "red" and "blue" voters could at one time or another be applied to the voters of the Iron Range. We are, on average, socially conservative, economically liberal populists who are averse to change, unless we decide change is needed, in which case we'll set fires in the streets if it comes to that. Then we'll complain about all the media that show up and block up the parking lot at the hardware store.

The first thing to know about Iron Range politics is that all the media-spawned conventional wisdom on "rural vs. urban" political trends should be cast aside. The Range is often considered to be a rural area by those who haven't spent much time here. But in truth, as Pam Brunfelt pointed out, the Iron Range is an industrial area, larger than Duluth but spread out over a long string of small-to-medium-sized mining towns. These towns operate much the way neighborhoods function in a large city, though these towns often act more like children fighting for a parent's affection, or, in the case of politics, money.

At the same time, parts of the Iron Range, such as the township where I now live in Itasca County and the township where I grew up near Cherry, are classically rural. But in all cases, you can't make the assumption that rural areas naturally break to conservative trends and urban areas naturally skew liberal. For instance, my home township, Balsam, tilted just slightly for George W. Bush in 2004 and is home to a strong evangelical Christian community like what you'd expect in a "red" precinct. But local DFLers, because of tradition and personal connections, still do reasonably well here. And then my native Cherry, which is one of the few legitimate farming communities on the Range, is solidly Democratic-Farmer-Labor. Meantime, the cities of the Iron Range are mostly 3-1 DFL towns.

People often wonder why Paul Wellstone did better on the Iron Range than anywhere else when his politics ran slightly to the left of most Rangers. The reason is because the Range will forgive political differences if people perceive the politician's motives as sincere and if the candidate visits often and listens well. So Wellstone thrived here while other liberals have not. It was telling that Wellstone died in a plane crash on the Iron Range on his way to attend the funeral of a friend and local political ally's father, an event that most U.S. senators would have skipped.

"Paul Wellstone inspired tears when he died," said Pam Brunfelt. "That was one of the most crushing blows to the Range. He had become, in a strange way, an Iron Ranger. We understood what he was about in a way that other people in the state didn't. He was about the common good, which mattered here."

To succeed in Iron Range politics, you have to know people, the area, and the history. Political conversations don't begin with "Do you support the Whatsit Bill?" They begin with "I was talking to Eddie Skavich the other day ... ya, he's Bobby's brother ... no they never did find Bobby's thumb ... ya, they found the finger. That was in Buhl ... so ya, are you for the Whatsit?"

Now, if you are good at the personal touch, it matters much less if you are for or against the Whatsit Bill and much more if you care about the people involved. Wellstone *actually* cared about people. Most of the good local politicians care, too. The rest are at least masterful in the art of talking down an angry bar mob.

My perspective on range politics is based on the fact that I've spent twelve years poking around the political structure of this place while covering, working for, and running campaigns. This began for me in 1996, when at age sixteen I learned about that year's race between Minnesota's improbable first-term senator, Paul Wellstone, and his challenger, former Sen. Rudy Boschwitz, the same guy he beat in a huge upset back in 1990. My parents voted, usually for opposite candidates (Dad for whoever the National Rifle Association liked and Mom for whoever the NRA didn't like). One time, when reading an encyclopedia as a kid, I asked my dad how old he was. I think he was thirty-two or something then. "Hey, you can run for the U.S. Senate!" I exclaimed. "I don't think so," he said. I was so disappointed. I had no idea why you wouldn't want to run for the U.S. Senate if you were old enough. So I was born with some odd genetic mutation that sparked political fires in me. In 1996, I walked in the front door of the DFL headquarters in downtown Virginia, Minnesota, and offered to help with the election. Wellstone won, and though I've been through more political defeats than victories since, I always muster enough enthusiasm to continue by thinking of that first campaign. With the exception of a year away for college and a short stint as a newspaper editor, I've been involved in "Range doings" ever since – organizing community events, advocating for causes, and serving in local political groups.

Now I'm twenty-eight (not yet old enough to run for the U.S. Senate, but old enough to know why dad didn't and I won't). I see few other twenty-somethings even thinking about participating in politics, or even basic community volunteerism. I go to bean feeds and organizational meetings and debates, to sit next to people my parents' and grandparents' age. I hear a lot about their kids who are my age and not there. There are more people involved who are my great-grandparents' age than there are people under thirty. That's not because there are no young people left on the Range, a popular misconception. It's just that most people my age who live on the Iron Range have very little to do with politics. Few have anything to do with their labor unions, if they have one. Young people vote, either based on their family's ideology, their professional ideology, or their religious ideology, but not as reliably as those of their parents' generation. I've only known a handful of under-thirty people, maybe half a dozen, who have run for the legislature, mayor, or city council in Range towns. As far as I know, all but one lost. The exception was the election of Tony Sertich to the State House of Representatives in 2000. Tony was the only twenty-something elected to a major Iron Range political office in a city or the state legislature since the mining depression of the 1980s when so many young people moved away. I was one of a cadre of young Iron Rangers working on his first campaign. To Tony's credit, he's worked his way up the ranks in state politics, becoming House Majority Leader in 2006, but we Rangers have to send a lot more young leaders up over the trench wall if we're going to survive our current crisis of apathy, economic disparity, and sluggishness.

The dearth of young in Range politics is deeply troubling from an historical perspective. Most of the effective leaders the Range has known, Democrat, Republican, or Independent, began getting involved in politics or their communities when they were in their twenties. That's not to say you can't start late, but *everyone* can't start late, or there will be a huge gap of leadership and organization on the Range.

If modern Iron Rangers fail to get involved in the shaping of our communities, we will squander all that our ancestors earned through blood and hardship. Part of the problem is that few of us know the story of how all of these political traditions began. If visitors bother to stop at our roadside markers, our historical societies, or Ironworld, they'd read stories about the early days of labor strikes, union building, and fighting the big mining corporations for a better way of life. From tales of the strikes of 1907, 1916, and the like, the conventional wisdom of Iron Range politics was born. This is when the distrust of corporations and outside influences, once only spoken in private, were voiced through political action. Further efforts in the 1960s and '70s allowed Iron Range communities to keep more of the mineral wealth for infrastructure and economic development. All of this work allowed the Iron Range to survive the devastating blow of the 1980s recession. We survive, quite probably because of these previous efforts by former Gov. Rudy Perpich, once an Iron Range state senator, his brothers who also served in office, and their political allies.

Perpich served as Minnesota's governor in two non-concurrent stints. He remains the Iron Range's most celebrated political figure.

After passing away in 1995, Perpich's name is hearkened in local politics as often as you hear of Ronald Reagan, John F. Kennedy, or Franklin D. Roosevelt. I watched my grandfather, who was not known for running, *run* into the street at the Keewatin Fourth of July parade in 1990 to shake Rudy's hand. Like Kennedy, Reagan, and Roosevelt, Perpich has the benefit in death of being revered by everyone, even those ambivalent toward his efforts while he was in office. Most holding an elective office of note on the Iron Range cite Perpich as a model for their service.

There was a boldness that sometimes shocked people about Rudy Perpich's politics. For instance, the Iron Range was deeply resistant to the peace movement during the Vietnam War, so much so that the Hibbing School District once paid for a long haired war-protesting high school boy, Larry Schleppegrell, to finish his education at a university. That same boy organized the Iron Range's first known Vietnam-era peace rally which drew about 100 people. The local newspaper refused to cover the rally, and most of the people involved were labeled hippies, agitators, or worse by outside observers. But the event did have one keynote speaker: Rudy Perpich, who was at the time a sitting state senator.

Perpich, his brothers George and Tony, and other officials led efforts to invest massive sums of mining money into our communities despite the strong opposition of mining companies. Now, such investment is expected, and mine bosses seek only to quibble about the cents per ton. *Newsweek* labeled Perpich "Governor Goofy" because of his eccentricities, bombastic persona, and big ideas. During his administration, Perpich spent an unprecedented amount of time concerned with Minnesota's role in the international economy. At the time, that was seen as overstepping his bounds or preening for national office; now it has become a standard part of the job description for modern governors. In short, he was eccentric, which seems like a requirement for Iron Range politicians, and a visionary, something decidedly *not* required of anyone to hold office here or anywhere else.

The work of the Perpich brothers and others has also allowed the Iron Range the enviable and sometimes dangerous luxury of being able to spend gobs of public money on economic development projects. Sometimes, that money is spent wisely for the economic diversification of the Iron Range and the improvement of our century-old communities. But money can and has been wasted for efforts that would do very few people any good. Personal political relationships, longtime practices, and the unsettling trend of former politicians becoming lobbyists-for-hire have sometimes clouded over what is truly best for our people.

But there's no problem in today's Iron Range that can't be solved with at least the same spirit of those early miners and organizers, if not their means and political affiliations. Whether Independent, Democrat, or Republican, today's Iron Range residents need to engage in solving the small and large problems of our communities. In doing this, there will be conflict and change, which our people have always simultaneously loved and hated. But I continue to believe that our area will face make-or-break challenges in the very near future, challenges of baby boomer retirements, fast economic growth sprinkled with large-scale failures, and continued loss of our region's storied political clout. It is my hope that the prevailing attitude of the early Iron Rangers has survived through the gauntlet of five generations:

We are here to work and raise families; but we have been pushed too far, so now we organize.

That's a tradition worth keeping. For our future to be a bright one, that tradition must endure.

State Quarter Decision
Worth More Than Two Bits

Hibbing Daily Tribune, August 2003

You've seen them. You might be collecting them. You're definitely aware of the collectable display cases sold on cable TV commercials.

I'm talking about state quarters. We all remember the excitement when the Delaware quarters first surfaced and the American public realized two great truths: "We have a state called Delaware?" and "Oh boy! My state will get a quarter, too!"

Well, here in Minnesota, our quarter is coming soon, and a committee is forming to decide what should go on our commemorative coin. The group consists of the very best students, teachers, coin experts, lawmakers, and private citizens who were willing to attend coin-related meetings.

State Representative Tony Sertich will represent the Iron Range on this committee. He was one of, well, one state lawmaker who clamored for the House of Representatives seat on the coin committee. Though the selection of a state quarter design might not be as important as a budget or economic development, Sertich does see more than twenty-five cents value in the endeavor. He said this quarter is a chance to educate the rest of America what our state is all about.

I'm sure a lot of folks have a lot of ideas for the quarter. Trees, loons, lakes, boats, and city skylines will be a big part of the discussion. Certain regions will push for farm equipment. Rangers might want a mine truck or big shovel. But maybe the committee could use some suggestions for a non-traditional coin.

We were all amazed when Alabama came out with their "Helen Keller" quarter. That was a real changeup. Then New Hampshire put a rock formation, the "Old Man of the Mountain," on its quarter only to have that craggy likeness of a man's face fall off the mountain a year later. Ouch. But it did draw attention to their state.

So here are some outside-the-box ideas for the committee. Take them or leave them.

Minnesota: Home of Post-It Notes

A lot of things were invented in Minnesota, but in today's office culture, the Post-It Note, developed by 3-M (which was founded in Two Harbors) stands tall. Even better, we could put a thin layer of adhesive on our quarter so that people could stick it places. OK, that might be a little too non-traditional. How about this:

Minnesota: World's Largest Ball of Twine

For a coin designer, the intricate, yet simple, look of the World's Largest Ball of Twine (which, as any good Minnesotan can tell you, is located in Darwin, Minn.) provides great fodder for a state quarter. Think of the detail involved in the individual strands of twine contrasted with the bold, single, round ball placed at the center of the coin.

If you're not a fan of twine, we have other options for you. Many of the state quarters already in circulation have a historical focus. They don't just represent their respective states, they teach people about them. So how about this:

Minnesota: They Drew the Maps Wrong so That's Why We're Not in Canada, Eh.

Yes, this is long. You could probably shorten it if you needed. But a lot of people might not realize that a mapmaker's error around the time of the French-Indian War moved the natural boundary between Canada and the United States. It was supposed to be the Laurentian Divide. If that had gone through, the Iron Range would have been smack on the Canadian border. What's that all aboot? Well, it beats putting Queen Elizabeth or a beaver on our coin, that's for sure, eh?

We've also got rich political history in Minnesota, so how about this fine quarter:

Minnesota: Where Mondale Beats Reagan

Sure, sure. It's a little political. But we were the only state to back former Vice President Walter Mondale in 1984 when he lost to Ronald Reagan in an electoral landslide. That makes us unique. We could have a picture of Fritz with his arm around the elderly lady from that really depressing two-minute campaign ad about Medicare that forced most of his supporters to curl up in the fetal position on Election Day.

Well, that's an idea. But we could also look forward to Minnesota's future with our state quarter.

Minnesota: Future Home of More Suburbs

As we learned in the last statewide election and legislative session, the ring of suburbs around the Twin Cities holds most of the power in this state. Census data also shows that pretty soon, central Minnesota will be part of the suburban ring, too. While our lone Iron Range representative on the coin committee might not favor such a design, the truth is that it might actually win in a statewide vote. Well, maybe if someone from Eagan suggests it.

The state quarters are released in the order the states came into the union. So our arch-nemesis Wisconsin, which formed in 1848, will get their quarter first. How about this? We float a fake design — something like a loon — until the time Wisconsin releases their quarter, which will probably feature cheese or the Packers. Then, at the last minute, we switch our design to the following:

Minnesota: Our Quarter is Better than Wisconsin's, and So is Our "You-Know-What"

You might ask, what's our "You-Know-What?" and the answer is, "whatever you want it to be." We're playing mind games with Wisconsin, that's all. It's like playing chess with a four-year-old. Just keep moving the pieces and tell them they're losing. It will be years before they figure it out.

Well, the committee has a lot of work cut out for it, so I'll leave it at that. If it gets too hard to decide, they can always play paper-rock-scissors or draw.

UPDATE: Our state quarter has since been revealed. It includes two anglers in a canoe on a lake with what is supposed to be a loon. In reality, experts agree that the bird is, in fact, a duck.

Fowl play is suspected.

Bicyclists in front of Hibbing's Androy Hotel

Pigeon and Squirrel Union
Could Cripple Hibbing

Hibbing Daily Tribune, July 2006

City hall and much of the downtown Hibbing area is facing an ongoing fight with pigeons, and, well, let's just call it "pigeon aftermath."

I don't know exactly when the war between the city and these disease-prone rat birds started. Some say it was when they closed the old hospital downtown, but wily veterans remember earlier man-bird skirmishes. Perhaps it all dates back to when legendary Hibbing mayor Vic Power strangled a pigeon on the steps of city hall, angering its 7,896 biological descendants.

Last week, a professional animal control person installed anti-pigeon strips to electrically "discourage" birds from roosting over the south entrance of city hall. Other discussions have centered around "hiring" a peregrine falcon to thin out Hibbing's pigeon flock. Though these tactics may seem extreme to some, anyone who has tip-toed around the white spots on the front steps of city hall knows what's at stake. If memory serves, we've already tried an owl decoy perched atop city hall. Maybe it really is time for some jolt strips or raptor muscle.

Pigeons, as many city residents know, are not the only small animal locked in guerilla combat with this Iron Range municipality. Every once in a while, squirrels manage to take down the city power supply when one of the furry rodents wanders into a high voltage area looking for nuts. I've joked in the past that PUC press releases regarding power outages should include a check box indicating whether the problem was squirrel-related or non squirrel-related. Well, I learned through one of my frequent perusals of the web that other towns experience such critter-induced power problems.

According to an AP story from Las Cruces, New Mexico, customers there lost electricity when a bird dropped a snake onto a power line. An El Paso Electric spokesperson could not comment on the size of the snake and "would not speculate on what type of bird dropped it." Also not included in the story was whether or not the "snake drop" was accidental or further evidence of a burgeoning animal militia testing its limits.

News analysts like to speculate about homeland security. When the government prevents an Al-Qaida terrorist attack by intercepting an e-mail with the subject head "Plan for Tuesday's terrorist attack," everyone is happy. So why isn't anyone upset that animals can randomly black out the grid? I'll even grant you that the animals probably aren't TRYING to shut down the wheels of commerce. I'm just wondering what kind of homeland security we can claim if we lose power when some wobbly old vulture whose eyes were bigger than its beak drops a sidewinder on the high tension wire.

Furthermore, what grisly conclusion could arise if the pigeons and squirrels began working together? Picture a dark night. Suddenly, the street lights are out. You hear it. "Coo! Coo! Coo!"

Then a splat noise, and another, and another. Your feet begin to slip. No traction anywhere! Aaargh!

So those concerned for our national security probably hope that peregrine falcon does a real Toby Keith number on those pigeons. For that matter, while the bird of prey circles our town – seeing all and knowing all – it can target squirrels, too. Perhaps then our long standing battle with small animals with high metabolisms will come to a successful end.

But I have a suspicion, as might anyone who's followed this cat and mouse game for the past few years, that the electric strips and hired birds are but an opening salvo in what might be a long, cold war with our feathered and/or furry friends. Buy a generator, durable shoes, and an umbrella. It begins.

Five Minutes

KAXE Commentary, November 2007

Fire! Flood! Robot attack! We can't predict what could force us to leave our homes in a hurry, but every so often, we're stricken by the news stories of people who face such woes. Most of these stories depict disaster survivors still in shock, holding precious family heirlooms or sometimes nothing. You don't always get five minutes.

With five minutes, what would I take with me? My list came easy. I have a small external hard drive that has all our computer files and family photos backed up. Our important documents are in a fireproof box. The scrapbooks are in the living room. Time permitting, I'd grab a few other photos around the house and maybe an old map hanging in my office that I couldn't replace.

Naturally, I told my wife about this list, and she shot me a look. "You wouldn't take your family!?"

Oh. My family.

Well, that's a given, isn't it? Doesn't that violate the spirit of the question? Now I'm the jerk who forgets the babies but remembers the external hard drive that has my iTunes on it. It's kind of like when you're asked what famous person you would want to be stranded on a desert island with, and you say, hypothetically, Angelina Jolie. So then you're the letch who cavorts with Hollywood starlets while your family waits by the phone for the Navy to call with news of what they presume will be the recovery of your water-logged corpse. Don't ask the question if you don't want to know. Would you rather I said Brad Pitt? It's just a question!

So, pictures and a hard drive. And my family. That's what I take with me in five minutes. The question shows how unimportant most of the things in our house really are. Most of it is replaceable. Lots of it wouldn't be missed at all. Recovering from any disaster is bound to be difficult, but I imagine it can be done easily so long as you have your family.

And your external hard drive.

In that order.

The DaRanger Code

(with apologies to Dan Brown,
author of *The DaVinci Code*)

Hibbing Daily Tribune, June 2006

Scene: The curator of the Iron Range Center for Art and the Humanities is found murdered with his body contorted into a ritualistic pose. Locals are alarmed to learn that there is an Iron Range Center for Art and the Humanities, it has a curator, and that the curator has been found murdered with his body contorted into a ritualistic pose.

Police are baffled by the many clues left at the scene of the crime, so they contact Robert Langdonich, a famous expert in Iron Range symbolism who happened to be in town because he never left.

CHIEF BOZO: Ya, Bobby, ah, what do you make of these numbers here on this naked fella's chest?

LANGDONICH: Looks to me to be a code, seven digits, probably a phone number. *(Dials number)*

CLERK: *(Answering phone)* Heavy Joe's Equipment Rental, would you like to hear our specials?

LANGDONICH: *(thoughtfully stroking former location of hair)* Yes. Yes, I would.

CLERK: We've got an imported plow. We're not sure where it's from. It's supposed to say "Till Sure" on the side but it actually reads "Tull Shur."

LANGDONICH: Tull Shur, eh? Is that an anagram?

CLERK: No, it's a plow.

LANGDONICH: Right. *(Hangs up)*. Quickly, to the HULL RUST Mine View!

CHIEF BOZO: Ah, Bobby. We're halfway through the column and you have yet to, ah, introduce the attractive female quasi-love interest.

LANGDONICH: We've only got 600 words. Are you willing to accept such a character without any sort of introduction or development, as though she were dropped from space with a preexisting understanding of everything around her?

CHIEF BOZO: Well, sure.

SALLY *(Granddaughter of the Curator)*: Robert, we must hurry!

LANGDONICH: Indeed!

(At the Hull Rust Mine View)

SALLY: Look how generations of mining changed the landscape of this area!

LANGDONICH: You think it was mining, do you?

SALLY: Well, I can witness actual mining operations currently in progress; look, a train carrying taconite to Duluth!

LANGDONICH: They may be mining now, but the mining during the Iron Range's early days was just a cover for something much more important. The early days of the Iron Range were rife with conflict. Warring gangs battled for control over the land. Of these, the strongest were the wookies.

SALLY: Wookies? Like from *Star Wars*?

LANGDONICH: Don't even get me started on *Star Wars*, but yes, we're talking about remarkably similar wookies. These wookies fed on the pure iron ore beneath the ground. When they seized control of this area, they conscripted conquered foes to collect it for them. One night, some of the humans got the idea to start selling the wookie food to Pittsburgh, and the trend caught on. Eventually, the wookies got hungry and lost their powers.

SALLY: If that's true, where are these wookies now?

LANGDONICH: Ever been to a county fair, or a street dance?

SALLY: Are you kidding; I'm from Chisholm.

LANGDONICH: Ever see a guy who kind of looked like a wookie?

SALLY: Yeah, you're right. I did!

LANGDONICH: There you go. If you need more proof look, at that sign over there.

SIGN: *"Wookies come and wookies go. Anagrams are hard to write on deadline. Sally, you're the last remaining heir to the wookie king!"*

SALLY: This explains so much about my sweater-like torso.

LANGDONICH: I thought it odd you were wearing long sleeves in June.

SALLY: I feel like I should have learned something at this point, but I'm not sure what.

LANGDONICH: Perhaps, Sally, we've learned that people will believe almost anything so long as the speaker sounds knowledgeable. If I look you in the eye and tell you that you are the only remaining heir to an ancient Iron Range wookie monarch, you might actually believe me. Especially if a lot of people buy a book that says that.

SALLY: But, it's fiction.

LANGDONICH: You can't spell non-fiction without "fiction," Sally. Think about it.

Son of a Gun

KAXE Commentary, November 2006

Once, someone asked my father why he chose to live in the country. He said he lived in the country because it was legal to shoot things off his porch. You can't do that in town. And dad was right. When you shoot things off your porch in a city, even the small Iron Range cities where we bought our groceries and school clothes, the neighbors call the police. When you shoot things off your porch in the country, your neighbors call you to ask if you hit it. If you did, they congratulate you. Cityfolk just don't understand.

I spent the first part of my childhood on our junkyard in rural St. Louis County and the latter part a few miles north, living in the shadow of a garage twice as big as our fancy new non-wheeled house. In both places, my dad shot things off the porch but more often shot targets from a decrepit old camper whose only purpose was to allow shooting during inclement weather.

My dad was not a casual shooter. His basement workshop was full of reloading equipment, and he spent many nights making shells that he would shoot off the next day from the camper. He was a collector. Two massive gun safes in the garage held a weapons cache that could have toppled the government of a small island nation. He started with hunting rifles, but later expanded into handguns and semi-automatics. Every month *The Shooting*

Times and a full spectrum of NRA publications arrived in the mail. Dad didn't exactly fear the government, but he didn't like it, either.

For my entire childhood, shooting was an escape for my dad. I'd get off the school bus, walk up to the house, the whole time hearing a steady cadence of gunshots, the tink-tink of shell casings against the camper's thin metal walls, and I'd know we were home, safe, and I would feel a sense of relief. I could stop wondering if the other kids liked me and start watching cartoons so long as the volume was loud enough to overcome the rifle blasts. When our family ran into money trouble, my dad sold most of his guns, one by one, to pay this bill or that. But you don't need a lot of guns to shoot; just one. And until the day I left for college, which proved to be the last day I'd live with my parents, the sound of gunshots was to me what the chimes of a grandfather clock would be to others.

Today, my dad still owns a small collection of guns but lives in an inner-ring suburb of the Twin Cities, the kind of place where porch shooting makes the news. I, on the other hand, live a half hour from everywhere, deep in the woods, where some days gunshots are the only signal that other people live within ten miles. I don't own a gun. But some days, sitting on my porch, I take comfort in knowing that I could shoot. I could shoot something right now, and it'd be OK.

Bob Dylan Drive in Hibbing

Bobby Zimmerman
Doesn't Live Here Anymore

Bobby Zimmerman doesn't live here anymore. He left the Iron Range in 1959 when he was eighteen.

Many Iron Range young people want to leave their small hometown for fame, fortune, or a different lifestyle in a bigger place. Even those who don't leave know the roads to take if they ever did. I may be a native Iron Ranger with no plans to leave, but I know State Highway 53 and I-35 very well. When frustration or longing run thick, I look down the highway knowing that a tank of gas separates me from a place completely unlike this one. When rural children become rural men and women, they must choose if they will ignore the bright lights of an urban existence that promises sophistication and variety. Usually, attending college in a city forces this decision between the ages of eighteen and twenty-three. Those still here at twenty-three usually stay for life. Those who leave at twenty-three sometimes come back, but usually not.

When Bobby Zimmerman left Hibbing, he knew he was leaving for good.

Like most ex-Rangers, Bobby visits, less often now that most of his relatives are gone. I hear around town that he keeps in touch with a few people he knew before he left. Most folks his age remember him, some fondly, most with indifference. He was a weird kid to some people, obsessed with blues and rock 'n' roll in a town that favored polka or country western.

Robert Alan Zimmerman attended the Alice Elementary School in Hibbing, which stood just a few blocks from the hospital where I was born. Both places have since been razed to make way for an assisted living facility and an independent senior community. Born in Duluth, Bobby grew up and graduated from high school in this mining town where his family ran an electronics store and a movie theater in the 1950s. Bobby was Jewish, living in Hibbing during the last generation when a strong Jewish community still existed. His upbringing was stable, his interest in music not especially unusual, and his talent at the time unremarkable. Two years after he left, 1961, Bobby Zimmerman signed a major national recording contract. Two years after that, he performed a folk concert at a packed Carnegie Hall in New York. Ten years after he left Hibbing, he had revolutionized American music and wrote songs that would influence many of the world's greatest artists, leaders, and writers.

Bobby Zimmerman changed his name to Bob Dylan after he left the Iron Range. *Rolling Stone* named him the second most influential rock musician in history, second only to the Beatles. His song "Like a Rolling Stone," is considered one of the greatest rock songs of all time. Dylan has been nominated for the Nobel Prize for Literature and in 2008 won a special citation Pulitzer Prize, the first rock 'n' roll songwriter to receive that honor. Still, a lot of people on the Range pronounce his name "Die-lan." The fact that Dylan left quickly and without any rosy tributes to his hometown is why it took more than forty years for Hibbing to offer any official acknowledgement of the most famous person who ever grew up there. It's also why the thousands of Dylan fans who make spiritual pilgrimages to Hibbing each year often report an unusual disconnect between the town and its famous son.

The story of Bobby Zimmerman, whose time in Hibbing was notable only for what he would later become, intertwines with my story. I was born in Hibbing and raised just a few miles away. My grandfather lived just blocks away from the Zimmermans when he was in high school. But that's not enough to make me the fan of Dylan that I am now. That story begins with me curled up in the fetal position in a Motel 6 hotel shower in Madison, Wisconsin, watching ivory tinted water flow down a hairy drain. It starts out about a girl and ends up being about Bob Dylan.

I was seventeen. I had a two-day break from my high school, and I was traveling alone through the Midwest, supposedly looking at colleges to attend the following year. In truth, I just wanted to go to Kalamazoo, Michigan to see a girl. Time would reveal that my parents' marriage was nearing its end, so when I asked to look at Northwestern University near Chicago by myself, my parents agreed, perhaps only to make one person in the house happy.

I woke early one morning, and, in the family minivan, journeyed 500 miles of U.S. Highway 2 across northern Minnesota, Wisconsin, and virtually all of Michigan, crossing the Mackinac Bridge, burning south on I-94 to Kalamazoo, another 500 miles.

I was in love. Not in the healthy, mature, Stephen Covey way that you're supposed to be in love, but in the seventeen-year-old way that is pure and passionate and doomed to failure. On the drive there, I heard Ray Charles' "I Can't Stop Loving You" for the first time, became entranced by its apt title and bold country/blues fusion, not hearing the pain in Ray's voice, not knowing that it was God telling me through the radio that I should have just gone to Chicago the regular way.

I met my friend, who was beautiful and who I very much wanted to be more than a friend to me. We roamed the campus of her college. I was a high school junior who had not attended the same high school she had, so my presence required an explanation to her friends. We had met two years earlier through a mutual friend, and despite her living eighty miles away from the Iron Range, I couldn't stop thinking about her. In fact, that distance was part of the allure. She was flirtatious and funny but also virtuous and proper. She was everything that I did not find on our Iron Range salvage yard, and her physical distance from me served to add a touch of the exotic for a young man who wanted to see the world. Through high school, we spoke on the phone, probably more than she wanted. She had a boyfriend for most of the time I knew her, but somehow that fact loomed as something that would inevitably change.

Now she was at college, and for two days, including two nights of me sleeping on her dorm room floor, we were together. I didn't have the courage to tell her that I loved her, but on the second day, on the shore of Lake Michigan, I managed to say that I thought I was falling in love with her, which was really more a matter of tense. She looked down, said "thank you," then paused. "I've only heard that once before." Another pause. "Maybe twice." More pausing. I meant it, I said. But she was a college freshman, and I was a high school junior. She was away from home for the first time, and I wanted to bring her home. The next morning I tried to kiss her goodbye and missed her lips. Her answer wasn't no; it was maybe, someday, but no day soon. I left Michigan, passing through the part of Indiana touched by the interstate. I toured Northwestern University in Evanston, Illinois, which was bustling with energy and prosperity. I knew that my family's failing business, my parents' failing marriage, my $400 savings account, and my dreams of becoming a journalist would all conspire to keep me from ever affording tuition there. I saw the happy people, and I was not one of them. All I could hear was Ray Charles, and he was sad, too. That night I stayed in a Motel 6 in Madison, Wisconsin. I tried to call my friend, but she was out. I took a shower at night so I could get up early to go home. I stood under the water for twenty minutes before deciding that I didn't want to stand any more. I slid down the grimy wall to the slick surface of the shower floor, curling up into a ball, unable to cry or stop loving her.

As Ray said in his song, they say that time heals a broken heart. For me, it was time and the Bob Dylan album *Blood on the Tracks*.

That album was recorded more than four years before I was born, about 200 miles south of where I grew up (rerecorded with a new band in Minneapolis after the first cuts in New York), and it was of course written and voiced by a man from the same town as me.

Die-hard Dylan fans don't need to be told facts about his background or albums. They have such matters filed away, deep inside their minds. I know this because from the bottom of that shower, I would begin a path that made me both a Bob Dylan fan and one of the organizers of "Dylan Days" in Hibbing, a long weekend of music and arts events held every May. My reason is, fundamentally, the album *Blood on the Tracks* generally, and the song "Idiot Wind" specifically. I listened to Dylan's music so much during that year after my failed search for the Northwest Passage of love, that the songs are indelibly linked to one of the lowest, most pathetic moments in my life, something I can't forget because failures like that are how one learns not to be pathetic.

I'm not a Dylan fan because I have firsthand memories of the 1960s. I don't think he's a prophet sent to save us from LBJ or Nixon. I don't think he's anything more than a poet and singer from the Iron Range. In 1997, "Idiot Wind" summed up how I felt when I got back from the Northwestern trip. "You'll never know the hurt I suffer, nor the pain I rise above; and I'll never know the same about you, your innocence or your kind of love and it makes me feel so sorry." He didn't write it for me. It was about his ex-wife and his feelings about some situation I'll never know. But I found that song, and inside I found a little piece of humanity that I could understand. From there, I began collecting his other albums, enjoying them for what they meant to me as I grew from a romantically inept high school student into a romantically inept college student who, mercifully for the world and my bounding heart, married young. And then there was this: I was ambitious, but unable to give up on my hometown and the region around it. Dylan did leave, but the fact that he was from here and became what he is, inspired me. Years later, when I was editor of the *Hibbing Daily Tribune*, I joined a committee organizing the first city-wide "Dylan Days," eventually heading the committee.

There's a bit of a generation gap in anything involving Bob Dylan. The crux of the problem is that people from my generation don't really care about the 1960s. This may be hard for baby boomers to understand. I care about the '60s, but no more than I care about the '30s. The only reason I consider either of them is because I follow history. That's right. *History.* Dylan's songs are thick with literary references and often so ambiguous that no two people could agree about their meaning. For a generation that flocks toward songs like "My Humps," listening to Dylan can be a lot of work. But I happen to think that young people from places like Hibbing, and other small towns, can find special importance in Dylan's story.

Bob Dylan was a middle class kid in a small place who came from a reasonably normal middle class family. Restless and curious, he longed for something big, but vague, on the horizon and used his love of music to get there. He grew up in a town that, one generation earlier, was ripped from its foundation and moved three miles south. He was Jewish at a time when most Jews were leaving northern Minnesota. He was young at a time when most young people were realizing that the mines couldn't hold them anymore.

In 1958, Dylan's band was laughed and booed off the Hibbing High School auditorium stage. Bob was singing a Little Richard song, pounding the keys of the school piano. It was the "Jacket Jamboree" talent contest. Depending on who you talk to, he was either terrible, or ahead of his time. The principal pulled the curtain out of anger or mercy, maybe both. Forty years later, I was dismissed as public address announcer during the national anthem before a girls' basketball game at Cherry High School. In my case, I was adding sarcastic jokes to the game introductions ("Good evening, ladies and gentlemen, and welcome to Cherry High School, where taking your first cousin to prom isn't necessarily a backup plan"). The coach was convinced that my comments distracted his players. I have always found affinity with Dylan on the matter of public performances at Iron Range high schools.

One year, I read the names at the Hibbing Community College graduation ceremony held in the high school auditorium. I'm a college teacher now. The auditorium is an historical site, the most expensive and ornate school hall in the country when it was built in the 1920s, a distinction that it probably still holds. To rebuild the auditorium alone would cost more than a brand new suburban school. It is the heart of Hibbing and irreplaceable. Those who see it for the first time are usually awe-struck, but students at the school hold no such reverence. "It's just the auditorium," one high school girl told me. "It's different when you go to school here." Perhaps, but for almost a century, Hibbing students have entered the world with the subconscious impression that the most important places in a community are where art, music, and education take place. That giant performance hall, draped with Czechoslovakian crystal, was the standard by which these students would ambivalently judge all future high school auditoriums. Dylan was one such student. He went so far as to mention the auditorium in his autobiography *Chronicles*. Our multi-purpose gym and stage at Cherry was no match, but even I could feel the power and privilege when I participated in events at the nearby Hibbing auditorium.

Like a Dylan song, Dylan's time in Hibbing is open to many interpretations. For instance, his high school English teacher, B.J. Rolfzen, tells everyone that Robert took special interest in poetry. Rolfzen might be the last person in the world who calls him Robert. Despite being an outsider who admired James Dean, Bobby Zimmerman sat in the front row of Mr. Rolfzen's English class in Room 204 at Hibbing High School. A copy of Zimmerman's essay on *The Grapes of Wrath*, marked up and graded by Rolfzen, recently sold for $34,000. In his concluding remarks on the twenty-two-page paper, Rolfzen wrote "I think that more could have been done with this, don't you?" I am one of several writers who have visited B.J. Rolfzen at his home in Hibbing, just a few blocks away from Dylan's boyhood home.

When you visit B.J. and Leona, you must first have coffee and dessert. You can try to refuse, but they will persevere. When that is done, B.J. invites you to his office in the utility room of his basement. In recent years, he has insisted that all reporters sit with him and listen to the Dylan song "Not Dark Yet" from start to finish. "To get us in the mood," he told me, as he tells everyone. "Not Dark Yet" runs six minutes, thirty seconds and B.J. knows every word. He taps his fingers at the same desk where he graded thousands of English papers from high school and community college students over a long teaching career, including Robert's *The Grapes of Wrath* report. Roughly speaking "Not Dark Yet" is about death, something that Rolfzen, at eighty-eight, worries about more than he used to. He comments on his age, but only occasionally and usually in reference to a poem. In all cases and in all subjects, B.J. prefers to talk about poetry. Rolfzen judged Robert Zimmerman highly as a student, mostly because he paid such close attention during poetry lectures in Room 204. B.J. will read a poem, sometimes falling into warm laughter or wiping a tear from his eye.

At first, you might think he is putting on a show, mugging for the reporters and Dylan experts who travel great distances to talk with him. But he has been like this forever. He would read and talk about poetry all day if you let him. B.J. has appeared during "Dylan Days" in Hibbing giving one of the same poetry lectures he gave Robert Zimmerman in 1957. He has given talks at large Dylan museum and music exhibits as well, in all cases proud of his most famous student. He often tells the story of when Bob Dylan came back to Hibbing for a family funeral in 2005. B.J. went up to Dylan to say hello, and after a brief chat, Dylan leaned over to him and said, "You taught me a lot." This line could be greatly analyzed by the critics, but B.J. believes that it's only the sign of a gentleman, something any old teacher would like to hear from a memorable student.

Many of the people who knew Dylan during his Hibbing years participate in "Dylan Days" now. In recent years, Dylan broke his silence on the subject of Hibbing in his book *Chronicles*, and now everyone seems to be more nostalgic and willing to talk. Leroy Hoikkala – drummer for the Golden Chords, one of Dylan's high school garage bands – was one of his best friends in school. For many years, he refused to comment on his years as Dylan's friend out of respect. Now he's loosened up a bit. Reporters often ask him questions about Dylan's mindset in Hibbing, what he longed for and thought about. Leroy told me they talked about music, and little else. That's what they were interested in and why they were friends. Leroy was on stage with Bobby Zimmerman during the famous "Jacket Jamboree" performance. He insists that many of the people were enjoying the show, but that the crowd was heavily divided.

That division, while softening, remains today. Not all voices in Hibbing sing praises of Bob Dylan. I worked with a Dylan classmate who would tell anyone who asked, "I wanted to kick Bobby Zimmerman's ass back in high school and still do." If you heard how he said it, you'd believe him (To be fair, he wanted to kick a lot of people's asses). Many others thought Dylan was, or later became, stuck up. And almost everyone in Hibbing knows and despises the fact that a young Bob Dylan claimed to have been brought up in a circus family that traveled the country, when everyone knew he grew up on 7th Avenue and his dad kept the books at Micka Electric. As a reporter, I did half a dozen stories on this topic, and as "Dylan Days" flak, I've helped about twenty different reporters write some version of this same story. Everyone wants to know why the town doesn't love Bob Dylan the way the media or the remnants of the '60s subculture do. I could offer theories, but I think it's just a part of being from the Range. We don't deal in fame or greatness all that often in northern Minnesota. All we ask is that when you speak of us, speak with respect. Dylan did not do that through much of the '60s and '70s but has lately. Perhaps that's why, in 2005, our "Dylan Days" group, thanks to the work of my friend Linda Stroback Hocking, was able to convince the city council and local residents to rename a portion of Seventh Avenue "Bob Dylan Drive."

One story that Leroy Hoikkala likes to tell is the time Bobby Zimmerman almost got run over by a train. They were racing motorcycles just north of Howard Street, the main drag, in an industrial section of town along the railroad tracks. A train was coming and, on the spur of the moment, Bob decided to race across the tracks before it passed the crossing. With engine blaring, Leroy says Dylan just barely squeaked across before the train, which was probably carrying coal to the utilities plant, steamed by. This story always made me wonder. The album that brought me to Dylan's music, *Blood on the Tracks*, could have been made literal in this mining town, long before "Bob Dylan" ever existed. When I lived in Hibbing, I would ride my bicycle almost everywhere I went, and sometimes liked to stop by the tracks on the north side and think about all the people who, with their stories, rolled through there on train cars or crossed the tracks in the other direction, perhaps just in time.

Dylan is Hibbing's most famous former resident, but he is not the one. NBA Hall of Fame basketball player Kevin McHale played for the Bluejackets, the University of Minnesota, and the Boston Celtics. Though I've yet to meet McHale, I've met members of his family and friends and did a newspaper story about their hunting shack several miles outside of town. He signed the thank you card along with everyone else in the group. Unlike Dylan, McHale is the model small town famous person. He makes frequent visits back to town, refers to Hibbing positively every time he's asked, and has done several local events, from junior high school appearances to gun safety clinics. When I was a kid, I saw McHale on *The Tonight Show*. He told a story about how he was playing a game and, sitting near the front row, he saw Bob Dylan. From what I recall, McHale was diving for a ball out of bounds, looked up and saw Dylan. Their eyes met for a brief moment. Dylan said one word: "Hibbing." McHale smiled back, and said "Hibbing."

So I keep my admiration of Dylan as reasonable as possible. Bob Dylan didn't save my life. He didn't make me who I am. I haven't met him and, though I'd love to, I probably won't. If I did, I imagine all I could really say to him is "Hibbing." He doesn't need my life details and I don't need his. This place is enough of a connection. Dig deep and you'll find a lot of love lost, pain, and conflict wrapped up in that word. You'll also find hope and a chance to move on and up. Up out of the lowest, grimiest shower stall. Up to where you want to be, famous or not, on the streets of Hibbing or on a never ending tour. For me, Dylan's story in Hibbing is really about unlocking the possibilities of life. A journey across a country, across a set of tracks, across a room to an unrequited love is worth taking, because that's what it takes to be human.

Hibbing's Bob Dylan
Now Selling Fancy Undies

Hibbing Daily Tribune, April 2004

If you hang around an Iron Range newspaper long enough, you're bound to encounter a well-dressed person lamenting that we print nothing positive in this here infernal rag. "Why don't you report POSITIVE news like you do all the negativity?" the impeccably groomed will say.

Well, now's the big moment. Nothing negative today, folks. Somebody from Hibbing – one of us – has been prominently featured in a Victoria's Secret TV underwear ad. Not many Iron Rangers get an honor like that (or become shamefully exploited by a leering, male-dominated sex industry, depending on your worldview).

Of course, that somebody is famed folk rock singer Bob Dylan.

Don't worry, Bob does not appear wearing the lingerie. Dylan does however get to ogle a healthy young woman wearing an angel outfit that just might slow your personal ascent to heaven.

Well, good for him. It beats most of my workdays, that's for sure. It does beg the question, though, why is influential poet musician Bob Dylan now selling ladies underwear?

I'm not the only person to ask this question. Columnist Seth Stevenson of State.com wrote an April 12 piece entitled "Tangled Up in Boobs" that poses an identical query. Stevenson came up with several possible answers, ranging from an unexplained need for money to pure Dylan whimsy. I like Stevenson's other theory, though. He writes, "I also wouldn't totally discount the idea that he's playing a sly, decades-in-the-making practical joke. Newspaper reports have noted that in 1965, when asked what might tempt him to sell out, Dylan said, 'Ladies undergarments.'"

Bob may have been following through on a thirty-year-old vow to show up that reporter. It makes more sense than Bob Dylan waking up one morning, spontaneously bellowing: "I shall endorse underwear today!" It also makes more sense than the marketing director of Victoria's Secret waking up one morning, shouting: "I've got it – we get Bob Dylan!"

I don't know how to sell lingerie, and I sure don't know how to buy it. Whenever I pass within ten feet of one of those stores I, become Lenny from *Of Mice and Men* ("It's pretty, George – Pretty!"). Thus, I dare not presume to know how women select their knickers. Until recently, though, I believed that Bob Dylan seldom influenced women's underwear choices.

That's why the Bob Dylan Victoria's Secret ad is all the more fascinating.

What's the message here? If you wear Victoria's Secret underwear, someone like Bob Dylan will ogle you? Or is the message really if you have a lot of money, you can look like Bob Dylan and still have half-naked supermodels trolling around your house? Either way, it seems to defy most standard marketing logic.

If you somehow missed this thirty-second underwear gem, you might be safe. It seems like one of those ads run only for a short time to get people talking.

Meantime, be proud, Hibbing. One of your own has reached new heights in the schilling of lingerie. And Bob, don't worry; you're still tops in my book. If this ladies' underwear experience doesn't make up for being passed over as a Nobel Laureate, I don't know what will.

Time to Dream

Hibbing Daily Tribune, September 2006

One thing I always liked about being from the Iron Range is that, when you run your fingers across the surface of a 3D relief map of Minnesota, you can find home in the dark. We're that ridge in the upper right. We're bumpy and red. So you can imagine my surprise to learn that the *The World is Flat,* according to Thomas Friedman's best-selling book of the same title.

The World is Flat details the rapid change in world economics over the past decade. It talks about how the outsourcing of American jobs, a hot button issue in politics, is part of a larger global shift that started when the Berlin Wall fell, continued through the dot-com boom, and is now only really getting started. Friedman concludes that we are moving into a world where borders matter far less than innovation; a world where people with more dreams than memories will harness technology for good and people with more memories than dreams will use technology to suppress change or do evil.

He comes back to that comparison – dreams and memories – often in the book's final chapter, and it instantly brought to mind my native Iron Range. Here on the Iron Range, memories are everywhere. Hibbing city fathers paved the streets at night to avoid the injunctions of the mining companies, who preferred dirt roads for their equipment. So and so was the first Catholic elected to the school board, the first woman to work as a laborer at a taconite plant, the first Iron Ranger to become governor. 20,000 people turned out to see John Kennedy at the Hibbing Memorial Building. We used to make kings. We won the war. Yes, memories are everywhere, and they make us who we are. But Friedman says memories mean nothing without dreams. I agree.

In *The World is Flat*, Friedman says the thing that separates so-called "terrorist states" from other developing countries is that these states have a combination of poverty and the suppression of dreams. In places like India, even in China, things are far from perfect, but young people are fervently seeking higher education and hold sincere hopes that they will do better in life than their parents. They want to start businesses, learn more, and improve their homeland. In case you forgot, that's how things were in America until just recently. That's how things were on the Range when it was at its peak.

You've probably heard that young people in our area don't dream about a future that includes the Iron Range. Most want to leave, we are told. Until recently, I'd have agreed. Many of the students in my classes at HCC had plans to transfer to a school out of the area and probably never come back, except to visit. But then a couple of weeks ago, I asked students in one of my communication classes to give a short speech saying what their goals were for the future. It was a class for students seeking a technical career. Most of these students had little interest in liberal arts degrees, and few would be interested in reading books by Tom Friedman. But it was these students who talked about starting businesses and growing new things here in northern Minnesota. It got me thinking. Why do so many parents celebrate sending their kids off to the Cities to earn $35,000 and live in a suburban apartment, and so few celebrate kids who want to try to grow new things right here at home? We need to start talking about homegrown innovation.

In the essay "What We Teach our Rural Children" by Paul Gruchow, the author encounters an old man who lives in his rural Minnesota town. The man asks Gruchow, a newspaper editor, what he has printed in his paper that "honored and protected the lives of his people." Gruchow could not provide an answer at the time, so he asks it of all of us. Friedman says we live in a rapidly changing world and can't stop globalization. But I say we can still honor and protect the lives of our people though innovation.

So I'll do what anyone should do when they hear a good general idea: try to make it specific. I'll write this column. Tomorrow, I'll go to work and do my best to honor and protect the lives of our people by encouraging new ideas. You'll probably go to work tomorrow, too. What will you do there? Maybe you think your job has nothing to do with the future of northern Minnesota, but I bet it does. If you have dreams, it does. Share your memories, but encourage your kids, and everyone you meet, to develop dreams. It's the only way this place and our people are going to make it.

What's Next for the Sons and Daughters
of the Iron Range?

Hibbing Daily Tribune, April 2007

At the center of every northern Minnesota economic development project, be it a power plant, steel mill, yarn factory, or plutonium mine, rests this argument: "We must do something to keep our young people."

On the Range, the term "young people" means those under forty – including high school and college students, young professionals, and families with small children. These folks are all lumped together because, demographically, the "average" Iron Ranger is a working middle aged person with older or adult children, or a retiree. Whether you're a twenty-eight-year-old lawyer with an engineer husband and two young kids, or a recent local tech college graduate looking for a job in the mines, you're the people economic development types want to attract or retain.

The Twin Ports of Duluth and Superior, Wisconsin, and the Iron Range have enjoyed a symbiotic historical relationship and are part of the same economic region. Though the two areas are not identical, they face similar challenges. That's why I read with interest a March 25, 2007 Associated Press story by Will Ashenmacher about a recent study relating to the attitudes of people who live in the Twin Ports area. The Duluth-Superior Area Community Foundation commissioned the study, whose findings were compiled by University of Minnesota-Duluth instructor Drew Digby with cooperation from the Harvard University John F. Kennedy School of Government. Among the findings were that young people in the Twin Ports are "highly involved, yet feel alienated from their community."

The study found that young people voted and participated in community service, but often felt a great sense of frustration. This was merely a quantification of something I have heard from many of my friends, that efforts spent to affect change or be creative seemed wasted in a place where tradition and parochialism reign in the end.

The report's authors said that part of the problem was that young people might not have an effective bearing on what it takes to be successful in civic engagement. I've seen that sometimes in young professionals who run for city council or school board offices but have no idea how to actually win the votes they'd need to be elected. But I've also seen good people pour their hearts into the arts, community improvement efforts, or civic groups only to receive little support for their work.

Our economic problems in northern Minnesota aren't a matter of having enough space. New mini malls, spec buildings, and business incubators are everywhere, and they're affordable. Our problems aren't really related to money. We have a business community here, and Iron Range Resources still spends millions every year on development projects. Our problems aren't related to politics. The Range reliably elects Democrats to office, but the Upper Peninsula of Michigan, a culturally and economically similar area, elects Republicans and faces the same issues as us.

Our problem is, in my observation, entirely related to attitude and geography. Indeed, we must attract and retain young people, embrace creativity, and forge new development. But we must then also accept changes to our economy and culture. We are out of the way, nowhere near a major population center or top tier national highway. Our natural resources cannot account for 100 percent of our existence anymore. Thus, we must give people an especially good reason to go out of their way to do business and live their lives here, something beyond pretty billboards and talk of good fishing. We can't count on homerun projects that employ hundreds to magically deposit their everlasting glory upon our doorstep. We must do the thinking, building, and working ourselves, by starting small and growing. This means entrepreneurship and innovation, using our natural resource strengths with our superior network of educational facilities.

This won't be easy, but it's the calling of the sons and daughters of the Iron Range. What can you do?

A Toddler, a Truck,
and the Theory of Relativity

KAXE Commentary, December 2007

So one day our son Henry, who was then two and a half, picked up a toy truck from the coffee table, examined it carefully, and made a simple declaration. "I've had this truck a long time."

We offered the standard parent agreement, "Yes, you have," while stifling laughter at the irony. He was two! Not only did his birth seem to happen yesterday, but I distinctly remember the day that truck came home, too. Grandma and Grandpa brought Henry back from a town trip, and he ran over to the coffee table, rolling his new truck back and forth with glee. The joy stemmed partially from the truck, but also from his realization that he now enjoyed full control over his grandparents when they took him to almost any store.

To me, not much has changed since that day. I'm on six different deadlines, our schedules remain packed, our twin boys Doug and George eat through Christina's homemade baby food like raccoons through a restaurant Dumpster, and Molly Dog continues to warn us of the looming threat posed by UPS delivery personnel. But that's my perspective, my "adult" point of view. At the same time, here amid the blue-gray demographics of the Iron Range, some still refer to me as younger than several pairs of their underwear, respectively. I have three children and a mortgage the size of Mothra, but whenever I go to community functions, someone always pipes up, "Oh, it's good to see the youth involved." I wonder how my perspective will change if and when I reach the golden years.

Albert Einstein once explained the Theory of Relativity this way: "When a man sits with a pretty girl for an hour, it seems like a minute. But let him sit on a hot stove for a minute and it's longer than any hour. That's relativity."

As my age clicks toward thirty, I can't complain much about time yet. Indeed, many of my contemporaries still live in their parents' basement wondering if any of these so-called "jobs" involve PlayStation. But a message in a Christmas card this year really hit home. Every year passes more quickly than the year before, my uncle warned. And it's true. Last summer my wife gave birth to the twins after Henry turned two and began talking in complete sentences. And then it was Christmas. Using Einstein's theory we'll be putting up the decorations for Christmas 2008 sometime next week.

I wonder about the time I wasted, back when time passed like a stone. During summer vacations when I was fourteen and fifteen, not yet old enough to drive or get a job, I whiled away the hot Iron Range nights in the basement where it was cool, eating peanut butter toast and sleeping on a ratty cot in front of an old color TV that got all four broadcast channels. I would stay up until all four networks signed off. After that, at three or four in the morning, I sometimes wandered bare foot outside in grass already wet with dew looking for the stars and planets from a late night astronomy show that had just ended. Every few weeks, the Northern Lights would arch above the tree line, over my dad's giant steel workshop, almost reaching the spot directly over our yard. I would go back inside, sleep until noon or one in the afternoon. Then I'd go for a fifteen mile bike ride to visit friends, eat dinner, and do the same thing all over again for three months. Today it feels like one tiny second in my life, but I believed those summers would never end.

Years later, our second floor apartment hovered in the eighty degree range all year round. Christina had to work weekend evenings, so I would spend hours playing computer games until ten, when I had a standing date to watch *Rocky and Bullwinkle* until she came home at eleven. I was twenty, an age many believe to be the prime of a man's life. This time, too, passed slowly. But with each accomplishment – a better job, a house, a better house, finally children – time accelerated. Today, each day feels like a blink, but leaves behind hundreds of memories; so many that they can't all be realized as they happen. Sometimes, I think I wasted those early years. How many books could I have written, languages could I have mastered? How much could I have learned about Gandhi or the Whiskey Rebellion that I currently do not know? But then again, in the life of a toddler, six months spent with a really good toy truck is a long time, a good long time.

That's relativity.

Life of an Iron Range Blogger

Website.

Web. Site. A site on the world wide web. The name implies place, but it's hard to find a place on the Internet. Oh, it's easy to get on the Internet and only slightly more difficult to create a website or blog. If the Web had an intellectual requirement it would be about as popular as modern jazz. It's much harder to figure out where the people who you find on the Internet are *from*. You don't usually see them and might not even know their names. The very nature of this ethereal universe that defines our modern era is contrary to the Iron Range tradition I've been talking about, a tradition that values knowing people and understanding the past. There is no past on the Internet, only the RIGHT NOW. Ironic, considering that everything that happens on the Internet makes an electronic footprint that will probably outlive the person who made it. News blogs shout and analyze the news of the day, occasionally lapsing into ancient history (last month). Personal networking blogs tell friends who I'm listening to, what I'm reading, and where I'm hanging out in the next few days. Modern? Think again. This is no different than my grandpa's coffee klatch, except that his group of old friends gathers every morning at ten at the Keewatin Sinclair station, and everyone knows each others' names, addresses, and life stories. When someone dies, everyone there goes to the funeral and their wives bring a casserole.

There are no casseroles on MySpace or Facebook. That's not to dismiss the exciting new possibilities of forming communities that transcend geographic barriers, but highlights that there is something important to human existence often missed in the blogosphere.

Yes, I am one of those blogger people. I started in 2006 because of dual realizations: 1) the Iron Range landscape I grew up in, physically, culturally, and politically, was still here, and 2) no one living in the modern oversized coffee group known as the Internet seemed to know what the Iron Range really was or anything about our people. And while the blog remains my single-biggest distraction from far more financially lucrative work, it has reinforced my love of the Iron Range.

For starters, I have found that Iron Range blog readers, though not great in number, still follow the speech patterns of Iron Rangers. In an e-mail, or even tapping me on the shoulder in public somewhere, readers explain who their relatives are, the places they used to work, the stories they experience, and how they know my family … and then what they thought about this post or that. I do the same on my blog, which might be a distraction from the general tone of many political bloggers, which is to simply blast a point so loudly as to drive the possibility of dissent out of readers' minds. And I find in writing for the blog that it feels so good to talk up the "us" values of public education, honest government, and a decent quality of life for people, and decry the powers of "them," everyone who gets in the way of those things. The speech teacher in me knows that there is a bit of fallacy in that approach, but it's one that is classically Iron Range. I don't know that one can ever banish that philosophy entirely.

Even in the Internet age, we should never forget the sense of place that makes us human. All of us are from somewhere. Where we're from influences how we think, talk, and act. No two people are the same, just as I am not a miner, but a writer, but most things I do are shaped by a truth that hovers above the horizon, even in my dreams.

Current mining operations at Hull Rust Mine View

The True People of this Land

Since I was old enough to hold my head upright, I've looked at the red piles of overburden on the Iron Range with wonder. At first wondered because of their unusual size and unnatural shape, and later, because I knew that they came from a mile below my feet, and that my great-grandfathers and all of my friends' great-grandfathers put them there. These overburden stores are piles of waste; low grade iron dirt that wealthy, powerful people didn't want. Yet these red heaps, some with touches of scrubby green plants on their sides like stubble, still make compass needles dance. On a clear, bright night, the moon will cast a glow on the overburden so it looks lilke a smooth and massive God-made hill. To look out at the Iron Range horizon is to gaze upon overburden: a landform created by people who longed only to exist.

My last name may not be ethnic and my family's traditions were almost entirely Americanized by the time I was born. But vestigial elements of the Iron Range story run deep in my veins, and probably in those of my three sons, who now crane their necks to look out the windows of our minivan at the big piles of overburden. Almost every Iron Ranger born today will hold only a dim knowledge of their immigrant background. Even so, every Iron Ranger, native or naturalized, should know that the Iron Range is a place that values hard work, education, community, and family.

I write this in 2008. And though I write about today, a book always sits on the shelf well past tomorrow. For the benefit of history, the word of 2008 is "change." Change in Washington. Change in St. Paul. Change in foreign policy. Change in the way we produce energy or cook French fries. Everyone is quick to point out that change is hard.

Perhaps it will not be as challenging on the Iron Range, a place that has known only change over its 100 years of modern history. Change happened drastically at first, then subtly, as our downtowns gave way to Wal-Mart, and our people looked to television for guidance, instead of the weathered faces of our Iron Range parents and grandparents. It's a familiar story, replayed in small towns, industrial centers, and rural areas throughout the nation. The Iron Range, isolated by its remoteness and tradition, has so far held off the homogenization seen in much of rural America. Despite even the negative changes, the Range remains a good place to live. If you expect it to be boring, it will be. If you expect it to be exciting, it can be that, too. It's basically a safe, (eventually) friendly, occasionally odd place to raise a family, get a great education, go to work, enjoy the outdoors, drink and/or pray. The innovation of taconite mining and the hit-and-miss successes of economic development efforts have allowed the economy of the Iron Range to remain alive. Our culture has remained intact because just enough Iron Rangers have been allowed to live their whole lives here doing largely the same things their parents did, believing many of the same things their parents believed, without the outside world enlightening or endangering their way of life. The rest of small town America, especially mining areas, were obliterated by progress. So the Iron Range still drinks its beer, shoots at deer, fishes when it can, votes straight Democrat, and regards this thing called the future with a feeling somewhere between indifference and marvel.

The future of the Iron Range, like its past, begins reliant on the land for its bounty and ends up defined by its people. Like most of my writing, I began this essay in a conversation. In this case, I was talking to a teaching colleague about this book and about how I intended to talk about the future of this place. "I know someone you should talk to," she told me. "He's a futurist, and he lives on the Range."

It's hard to get people to talk about the future here. Iron Rangers have two ways of looking ahead: 1) How am I going to get through next winter? And, 2) which kid gets the snow machine when I die? An Iron Range futurist could knock down the future prediction business quickly and save me a lot of trouble.

"He's retired, but you can tell him I said to call you," my colleague said.

A retired futurist? How does one retire from looking to the future? Do you just stop writing it all down? Do you keep reading the same chapter in a history book? Or do you look ahead, and silently endeavor to cause the opposite to occur? I had to find out.

I met with Dr. Courtney Peterson, a very calm retired psychology instructor with a distinguished silver-specked beard. Though not a native, Peterson had moved here during the Vietnam War to take a job, returned after he was drafted and served in the war, and stayed after retirement, the mark of someone who has adjusted to life on the Range. Not comfortable with the moniker of "futurist" (his specialty was *educational* futurism), he did talk about interesting trends that, while not as secret or Nostradamus-like as I had hoped, provided some insight into the possible future of this area.

Forest products, both existing and yet-to-be developed, could energize new biofuels that would revolutionize transportation, heating, and electricity. The huge demand for raw materials could keep iron mining and other forms of mining going far longer than expected, perhaps another century. And with the prospect of global climate change threatening existing ecosystems, a shortage of fresh water could make our lakes and aquifers as important as an immense oil field would have been during the Harding administration.

"The basic economy will simply be expanded, and you'll see the possibility of other industries and vocations as telecommuting becomes more viable here," said Peterson, who also said that the region's geographic distance from major population centers could be negated by the wider use of existing technology.

While Peterson provided a great conversation about the future of the Iron Range, it became evident that it would take much more than one educational futurist to get the whole picture. I received another tip when KAXE, a local independent radio station, hosted a discussion session inviting citizens to share their thoughts and visions about the future of the region. Sponsored by the Meadowlark Project, a think tank that works with communities around the Northern Great Plains to affect a better tomorrow, this gathering brought many kindly northern Minnesotans to the Grand Rapids Public Library. They talked about what was good and bad about northern Minnesota, exploring possible scenarios of the future filled with so much elaborate detail that they would have seemed real if they weren't all so different. Most of them involved the idea that our natural resources could be better harnessed for the modern world.

Any attempt to predict the future boils down to the same kind of conjecture that led the Itasca County Historical Society to

declare in its 1960 Itasca County publication *Mines, Pines and Lakes*
that: "Tomorrow, with atom-powered plants, electricity will be so
cheap it would be shameful not to use it for almost everything.
Companies may charge a flat annual rate rather than a KWH rate.
Itascans will develop strong calloused thumbs to push buttons"
and that the county will boast important "machine-operated
farms." The book even says that the future will include "one or two
broad new highways" that stretch "smooth and straight, north and
south, east and west through the county" and whole region.
Amazingly, futurists of 1960 seemed even more futuristic than
those of today. We're still waiting for that "one or two broad new
highways" up here.

Even cynical, battle hardened Rangers recognize the reality that
the Iron Range will "survive" in some form well into the future.
We have iron ore, the forests, and fresh water.

What will the Iron Range be like for those who will live here?
Will our culture represent the best hopes of our immigrant
ancestors and the workers who literally built the mountains on
which we now stand? Or will our culture simply represent what
remains after a century in the hard sunlight of globalization,
political apathy, and too much beer? These are large queries that
confound futurists. And me.

Pam Brunfelt, who has given me so many great ideas about the
past, also shared a phrase from another historian that sharpened
my perspective on the past, present, and future of the Iron Range.
The phrase, quoted from Ralph Harney's booklet *Entrepreneurs and
Immigrants,* a publication for the Iron Range Resources and
Rehabilitation Board, comes from the Slovenian word *tuteshi,*
meaning, "We are the true people of this land." Marvin Lamppa
believes this statement is the rallying cry of Iron Range history. I
think it's also the rallying cry of our future.

The Finns, Italians, and other Europeans came to mine the Iron
Range long ago, among them other lines of my convoluted family

tree. They came after mound builders, Dakota, Ojibwa, French Voyageurs, and loggers had already declared, with both passion and futility, that they were the true people of this land. Nevertheless, no one could stop these immigrants. They were hungry, looking for something the Range offered: a home, where there was steady work and opportunity for their children. And land. In Finland in particular, there was no honor quite like owning land. The first generations of these immigrants did not own land. They worked underneath it, bleeding and dying in terrible conditions. Though no papers declared them the owners of this place, they began to feel that they owned it anyway. They owned their tools and the clothes on their backs. They even had to buy the candles for their helmets. So they organized. When the powers of the steel trusts and the local bosses lifted their boots to stomp out the movement, the call would have been largely the same. "We are the true people of this land."

As each wave of change washes over the rock of this place, each wave shapes what we see today and will see tomorrow. The waves are nothing more than people willing to come here, stay here, and live and die here. They will come from places unlike this one. Some will come to mine, but most will come to do any number of other jobs – jobs that our parents and grandparents would never have imagined possible. Jobs that may not yet have been invented.

The true people of this land weren't chosen by a mining company, the government, or even God. We chose to live here. Despite all the barriers and hardships, the people who live here and who will live here in the future choose this life. I am proud to live on the Iron Range. The early decades of the 21st century promise more potential for growth, change, and improvement to our quality of life than any other time in our history. Modern life on the Iron Range is not for everyone, but the modern Iron Range is ideal for people who work hard, expect the same of others, and demand better for the generations that will one day take our place.

The Iron Range is not immune to the pressures and trends of the country and world at large. Indeed, we are a living example of how a place that seems average affects the world in a million unseen ways. Our rough towns defeated tyranny in World War II and fueled the rise of American power in the 20th century, while today, they subtly fuel the rise of India and China in the 21st. Our attitudes about banding together to lift our kids to a higher quality of life helped shape the state's politics, tilting countless Minnesota elections toward the growth of the nation's best schools and colleges. Indeed, we are not average. Our horizon does not contain skyscrapers, monuments, or mega malls, but instead, we gaze at overburden, which is not picturesque so much as it is ours. Ours. In that spirit, for the sake of my children and those of my friends and neighbors, I am happy to affirm that we are the true people of this land.

Bedtime

My sons are sleeping upstairs in their room. Henry, who is three, read a *Curious George* book with me tonight before bedtime. It was from an anthology of the famous children's stories from the 1950s. Of course, most of Henry's knowledge of Curious George comes from the TV show that airs on PBS, which features many of the same stories with a more diverse, modern cast. But the original book still holds its charm. We got to a part about Professor Wiseman, the director of the science museum, who in the book is a grey-haired white man, but in the TV show is a younger African American woman. When Henry pointed at the man and asked, "Who's that?" I said, "Professor Wiseman." He said, "No it isn't." All I could say was, "This is a different Professor Wiseman. This is Professor Wiseman's dad." "Oh," he said. It made sense to him.

After a while, it made sense to me, too. The story holds up just the same.

Doug, almost one, is too busy for stories most nights. He listens, but after a page he is raring to go explore. When he hits the sheets, he even sleeps hard. His brother George, almost one as well, was upset tonight. He is going through that time in a baby's life when he wonders if mom and dad are ever going to come back.

It occurs to me that one day, I will be a name on a dusty list of ancestors, like the one that sits in my desk drawer today. "Brown Family History" reads the manila envelope. My life is not fully contained in that envelope yet, but one day it will be. So what is the point? What is the point of living and dying in a place like northern Minnesota? Or any place, really?

The point is to live a story. To be a hero who, despite flaws and mistakes, tries to do good. To explore life, not just through expensive travel or artificial experiences, but through finding who we are and what we can be. And then, most important, we must tell the story. To our kids. To someone. We are a people of stories. Stories need settings, though, and there is no setting quite like the Iron Range, where I was born and live today.

Aaron Brown

Aaron J. Brown is a writer, community college instructor, and political organizer from northern Minnesota's Mesabi Iron Range. He writes a weekly column for the *Hibbing Daily Tribune* and weekly commentaries for 91.7 KAXE, Northern Community Radio, in Grand Rapids, MN. Brown grew up on a family-owned salvage yard, graduated from Cherry High School, and holds bachelor's and master's degrees in Communication from the University of Wisconsin at Superior. He lives in Itasca County with his wife Christina, sons Henry, Douglas, and George, and a loud, barking dog Molly. He is the founder and editor of the Iron Range's fastest-growing news and commentary blog, MinnesotaBrown.com.

Author's Acknowledgements

This book includes material from 2002-2008, but was put together in 2007-2008, just as our twin sons were born. This happened to be the busiest twenty-four-month period of my existence (so far) and it feels good to finish.

First, I thank the many people who contributed directly or, more often, indirectly to the idea of this book. Pam Brunfelt, my colleague at Vermilion Community College, provided invaluable perspective on Iron Range history and sociology that shaped key themes. Heather McLaughlin, formerly of the Hibbing Historical Society and Craig Hattam also provided important historical stories and context. Lisa Vesel, Courtney Peterson, Dan Jordan, Bill Schleppegrell Sr., Norma Schleppegrell, Bill Schleppegrell Jr., Tony Sertich, and Tom Anzelc contributed valuable perspective to specific essays. And many others were instrumental to the columns and essays that were republished here. I owe much to the many friends and colleagues, both on and off the Iron Range, who asked the questions that helped me focus this book. I also leaned quite heavily on the research on display at Ironworld and published in Marvin Lamppa's *Iron Country*. Please rely on these sources, not me, for the comprehensive history of the Iron Range.

I thank all my Iron Range teachers. Anyone who taught at the old Forbes Elementary in the 1980s (which is now the Boondocks Bar) or Cherry High School in the 1990s is partially responsible for my love of writing and teaching. I couldn't fit all the names of the people who encouraged me at this time of my life, and I can only hope that my kids are one day blessed with teachers and staff like the ones I knew. I also thank the radio news directors that provided important guidance at an important time: Cindy Kohlmann, formerly of KDTH in Dubuque, Iowa, and Mike Simonson of KUWS and Wisconsin Public Radio in Superior. Creative writing professors Anthony Bukoski and Barton Sutter from University of Wisconsin-Superior deserve recognition, as do many of my other UWS teachers and friends on the staff of the Promethean newspaper.

I thank the staff of the *Hibbing Daily Tribune*, especially Terese Almquist who hired me as editor, encouraged me during hard times, and allowed me to continue writing my column when I left for graduate school. I also thank her successor, Wanda Moeller, for agreeing to release my columns for this book and for her continued support.

I also thank my many colleagues at Hibbing Community College along with my fellow volunteers in the "Dylan Days" group, especially Joe and Mary Keyes from Howard Street Booksellers and Bob and Linda Hocking from Zimmy's.

It's been an honor to write for 91.7 KAXE, the gem of northern Minnesota media, and I'm happy to share some of that writing here. I thank Scott Hall for first inviting me into the KAXE world. I also offer sincere thanks to my producer and friend Heidi Holtan, whose editing and support continue to improve my writing and whose help with this manuscript is greatly appreciated.

I thank Lindsy O'Brien, the editor and publisher of this book, and Red Step Press for the opportunity. This idea materialized a long time ago, and Lindsy has shown both tremendous drive and patience in turning straw into a somewhat less straw-like substance. She is a good friend and a trusted ally in the fight to make northern Minnesota a better place.

Finally, I owe all else to my family and friends, both off and on the Iron Range . To my parents, Ward Brown III and Sandra Johnson, who taught me to love books and encouraged my writing, even though I must have perplexed them. To my sisters, Alyssa, Amanda, and Tori, who shared the experiences of growing up "Brown." To my grandparents, great-grandparents, uncles, aunts, cousins, miscellaneous steps, halves and vague kinfolk – your collective stories make me who I am. To the friends of my youth and today. And, to my father- and mother-in-law John and Jan Hiatt, whose support and internet-free basement meant much to me and this book.

And, most of all, to Christina, who makes me a better man, and my sons, Henry, Douglas, and George, who I hope will one day reach higher and farther than I could ever imagine.

I love you all.

Publisher's Acknowledgements

Red Step Press would like to thank the following:

Kelly O'Brien of Silver Pine Design (www.silverpinedesign.net) for designing our company logo and taking the cover photo for Overburden;

Graphic Designer Christie Culliton for laying-out and designing the cover;

Readers/editors Anna Jacobson, Lauren Lundeen, Jill Lyman-Lusche, Jonathon Muckala, Becky O'Brien, Kelly O'Brien, and Shannon Smith for their thoughts and expertise on the manuscript;

And Aaron Brown, for giving Red Step Press the opportunity to publish such a fantastic book on our first time to press.

Photo Credits